Drama, Literacy
and
Moral Education 5–11

Drama, Literacy and Moral Education 5–11

Joe Winston

David Fulton Publishers
London

David Fulton Publishers Ltd
Ormond House, 26–27 Boswell Street, London WC1N 3JD

First published in Great Britain by David Fulton Publishers 2000

Note: The right of Joe Winston to be identified as the author of this work has been asserted by him in accordance with the Copyright, Designs and Patents Act 1988

British Library Cataloguing in Publication Data
A catalogue record for this book is available from the British Library

ISBN 1–85346–636–0

Typeset by Textype Typesetters, Cambridge
Printed in Great Britain by The Cromwell Press Ltd, Trowbridge, Wilts.

Contents

Acknowledgements   **vii**

Introduction   **ix**
The structure of this book   xii
How to use this book   xiii

1 Schemes of work   **1**
Year 1: Traditional tales and fairy stories: The Frog Prince   1
      Other drama activities for work with traditional tales   8
Year 2: Tinker Jim   14
Year 3: Sho and the Demons of the Deep   27
Year 4: Sweet Clara and the Freedom Quilt   37
Year 5: The Sea Woman   56
Year 6: Macbeth   72

2 Planning for moral education through drama   **93**
Positioning drama in the moral education curriculum   93
The moral power of enacted narrative   94
  Objects   94
  Objects in space   95
  Sound   96
  Movement and stillness   96
  Teacher in role   97
  'Acting responsibly'   98
Games, rules and drama   101
  Games and rules   101
  Drama and rules   102
  The game of drama   103

Dialogue, dilemmas and passionate reasoning   104
  Reason and emotion   104
  Dialogue as action   106
  Different points of view   106
Drama as a public and communal forum   107
  The cultural and communal nature of moral values   107
  Social roles and the virtues   108
  Drama and the public sphere   109

3 A whole-school framework   **111**
A framework for literacy   111
A framework for drama   118
A framework for moral education   119
Documenting objectives and assessment criteria   122

Appendix 1 Games used in the lesson plans   **124**

Appendix 2 Drama conventions referred to in this book   **126**

A short bibliography   **129**

Acknowledgements

First of all, I must thank the teachers and pupils of the following schools:
   St Augustine's Primary School, Kenilworth
   Whitmore Park Primary School, Coventry
   Woodloes First School, Warwick
   Overstone Primary School, Northants.
They allowed me to try out and test the schemes of work presented in this book and were always welcoming, energetic and fun to work with.

In addition, I would like to thank the following people:
   my wife, Gill, for her encouragement and support throughout this project and for the conception and design of the finger puppets;
   Hilary Minns for reading early drafts and offering her invaluable words of advice;
   Miles Tandy for reading later drafts and offering *his* invaluable words of advice;
   Jonothan Neelands for his advice on the *Sweet Clara* drama and for lending me his copy of *Tinker Jim*;
   Femke Blackford for allowing me to build on her original ideas for *The Frog Prince* drama.

Finally I would like to thank all the teachers who took part in the Drama and Literacy course at Warwick University during the summer term of 1999. Their enthusiasm, lively good humour and willingness to try out the material in their own classrooms proved to be as informative for me as it was reassuring.

Introduction

Since before modern schooling, before literacy itself, stories have been told in every culture not only as a form of entertainment but also as a means of transmitting values from one generation to the next. Narrative story can be seen as one of the fundamental ways in which the human mind interprets and speculates upon the world and translates lived experience into conceptual understanding. Stories about the origins of the world, of a people and its culture, of heroes and heroines, of tricksters, fools, and animals that transform into humans, of love, fidelity, loyalty and death – such stories have always provided the framework for looking at and understanding the social world in which human communities have variously but continuously existed. As such, for adults and children, they are maps of possible experience, of the paths our lives might take if we are fortunate or unfortunate, virtuous or vicious, conformist or rebellious. Their moral significance lies in the models of action they propose and in the frameworks for moral thinking and ethical judgement they provide. Stories might suggest role models, such as in the Hindu tale of *Savitri*, or give lessons in pragmatism, such as the fables of Aesop and the *Panchatantra*. They might urge the value of particular moral virtues, such as in the tales of Jesus, or they might suggest a more ambivalent moral purpose, as in the Sufi tradition, where listeners are expected to glean a different meaning from every hearing, depending upon their changing circumstances. But in each case, a good story not only captures its audience but also suggests to them how their own lives, and those of others, might be lived. It is in this broad moral sense that stories are best appreciated as carriers of moral values, rather than being conceived of as illustrative of simple moral rules. Traditionally, societies have valued stories more for their ability to structure and develop the moral imagination rather than for their potential to develop literacy.

For primary teachers, the idea that stories can have a moral function probably calls to mind the school assembly, where they all too often become the prelude for a piously didactic homily and are often chosen not for their power but for their economy of length and simplicity of focus. Such stories are seldom seen as models of storytelling, as exemplars of language use or as stimuli for exciting possibilities in other curriculum areas. But the many good stories of whatever genre that do present themselves as vehicles to develop literacy, whether short stories, picture books, traditional tales, recent or classic novels, will very often present equally exciting possibilities for moral learning.

The National Literacy Strategy, introduced in England in 1998, recognises the power and importance of stories. A wide variety of fictions and genres of fiction are at the heart of the range of work it recommends. However, its list of overall objectives and termly targets emphasise technical competence rather than the development of the moral imagination. And, although the discussion of plot, character and theme are seen as of central importance, no rationale is provided as to *why* fictional stories are important, as to *what* children learn from them outside the objectives of literacy. Any benefits that stories bring beyond technical literacy itself are implied rather than made explicit. Of course, schools and teachers retain the freedom to choose stories for purposes beyond the acquisition of technical literacy, crucial though that might be. The danger is, however, that the moral learning potential of good stories might be sidelined, especially as discussion time within the literacy hour is explicitly geared towards comprehension, composition and word level work such as phonics and spelling. Within such limits, limits of time as well as objective, there is a danger that stories might be used *only* as vehicles for literacy, just as stories in assembly are often used only as vehicles for reinforcing simple moral rules – that stealing is wrong, that generosity brings its own rewards, etc.

A good place for dwelling within the moral world created by good stories may well be away from the pressures of the literacy hour; and a good way to explore the moral discourse of such stories can be through drama. For drama, too, operates through the medium of story, particularly within the primary years. Drama is essentially a form of communal story sharing, an art form far older than the literary novel, operating principally through an oral and physical medium rather than a printed one. As such, it can provide space for the kind of speaking and listening signalled as important by the National Literacy Strategy. Furthermore, whilst meeting its own learning objectives, it can reinforce those aspects of the literacy strategy that aim to develop children's understanding of theme, character, plot; and – crucially – this can highlight the moral content of the fictional story world. Because its mode of representation is different from the literary medium, using the body, speech, objects, space and light rather than print upon a page, drama can complement as well as reinforce the story work of the literacy hour. It allows children to use alternative intelligences, alternative literacies in addition to those of print – the visual and the kinaesthetic, in particular. It thus enables them to achieve understandings they might otherwise find difficult or elusive. Added to this, we must not forget that children receive most of their stories these days *as drama* of one form or another, particularly through the media of video and television. Most people today are introduced to the classic novels of Jane Austen and George Eliot, for example, through the medium of television drama; and just as this usually leads to radically increased book sales, we can use drama to 'turn on' primary aged children to the pleasures of a good story book.

None of this is meant to imply that any linkage between drama, literacy and moral education will be necessarily simple and straightforward when it comes to classroom practice. Numerous possible problems can await us, as I can illustrate with reference to a lesson from the best-forgotten past of a well-respected colleague, who is happy for me to recount this tale from the days when she was a student teacher. Having told a class of Year 2 children the tale of *The Good Samaritan*, she discussed its theme, which she herself defined as 'Be nice to one another', before asking the children to get into groups, choose a part of the story and act it out. Whereas a group of three girls spent their time playing nurses, fetching tea and bread and butter to one another and bandaging each others' arms with their scarves, a group of boys thought it more fun to act out the scene where the robbers ambush and beat up the victim. In fact, they found this to be such good fun that they also ambushed and beat up the Samaritan. This left the teacher rather uneasy, but at least they were enjoying themselves, she thought. After the dramas were shown, however, she felt compelled to reiterate the message of 'Be nice to one another' before lining the children up for playtime. Two minutes later one of the little girls came crying to her, complaining that one of the boys had kicked her on the way into the playground.

With the easy wisdom of hindsight and after many years of reflection and experience, this example still raises a number of issues. Firstly, the choice of story and the interpretation of its moral. *The Good Samaritan* is not essentially a tale urging us to be nice to one another; it asks how far we will go to help those whom for one reason or another – whether through race, nationality or social class – we may not be inclined to regard as 'our neighbour'. As such, it poses the question 'Are we as good as we think we are?' This is all rather complex for six-year-olds, of course, but, at the time, my colleague had not herself read these meanings into it. In the search for a moral lesson, she could think of nothing more profound than that, if we were all nice to each other, the world would be a better place. She lacked any guidance as to what might constitute suitable moral learning for young children and how she might effectively go about teaching it. Finally we need to consider the inappropriateness of the drama exercise. In making a virtue out of choice, the result was stereotypical gender behaviour far removed from the theme of the lesson, for the boys at least. The fact that these boys failed to respond to the piety of the message was painfully evident (literally) in the behaviour of one of them as he left the classroom.

The anecdote highlights several issues that remain pertinent if we wish to use story and drama for the purposes of moral education:

- as teachers, we need guidance to help us plan the content of a moral education curriculum;
- when choosing a story we must be clear that it establishes a moral agenda appropriate to the age range, social development and interests of the children;
- if this agenda is too pious or overly didactic it will probably lead to poor drama work and poor moral education;
- we need to be clear about the variety of drama activities open to us;
- we must be careful not to *ab*use a good story.

This book is designed to address these issues within the context of the current concentration on literacy. It does not seek to criticise or subvert that drive in any way. Rather, it seeks to help primary teachers use selected stories not only to develop literacy but also to plan for drama work that can harness the potential for social and moral education, itself an area under increasing attention from central government agencies.

The structure of this book

The book is divided into three sections:

Chapter 1

This is by far the most extensive chapter and contains the details of six drama projects, all of which have been successfully trialled in primary schools. Each project relates to a specific year group and is aligned to a selection of literacy targets prescribed for a particular term. Each contains:

- *A list of the literacy objectives and social and moral themes covered by the work.* The former are taken from the National Literacy Strategy, the latter are for the most part drawn from the Citizenship Foundation's publication *You, Me, Us!* which I discuss in Chapter 3.
- *Details of the story at the centre of the project,* including a summary of its plot; publication details; and a rationale for its inclusion in this volume. I have tried to vary the stories vis-à-vis genre, cultural origin and the type of drama work and moral learning they might generate.
- *A brief description and rationale of the drama work.* Over the six projects I have tried to cover a broad sample of drama activities, ranging from 'living through' dramas guided largely by the teacher in role to lessons that concentrate on developing children's performance skills. These are meant to be illustrative of a more or less complete drama curriculum for primary children at various levels of progression. The one noticeable absence from this curriculum is the area of script work as I judged it not to tie in so readily with the area of social and moral education.
- *Organisational details,* including time-scale and timetabling implications.
- *The sequence of drama lessons.* These are presented in lesson plan format, with clear objectives for both drama and moral education; a list of any resources you will need to teach them; a detailed description of the sequence of proposed activities; and assessment criteria that relate directly to the lesson objectives. In the lesson plans for Years 4–6, the sequence of activities is divided into two columns, with the column on the right consisting of a commentary, offering advice and possible variations. Throughout the plans, certain words are printed in bold type. These refer to specific games or particular drama conventions that are given in a glossary at the end of the book.
- *Questions for discussion/circle time.* Discussion often happens in drama lessons but, as access to hall space can be very precious, you may well wish to reflect on some of the drama work back in class. Circle time can offer a valuable opportunity for children to make connections between their own experiences and what happens in drama time. The questions here are designed to help children articulate and discuss the moral themes that are listed as learning objectives.
- *Links with literacy objectives.* Here the specific literacy objectives are listed with details alongside of how either the drama work itself has been meeting them; or how various activities that can emerge from the drama lessons can do so.

Chapter 2

Here I attempt to describe the various ways that drama can promote social and moral learning. My intention is to offer a theory that can help you plan your own drama lessons with learning objectives in social and moral education. I use examples from the six projects to illustrate my arguments and, at the end of each section of the chapter, I offer brief pointers to assist with your planning.

Chapter 3

In this brief, final chapter I present a straightforward model as to how you might chart the learning objectives for each project in each of the three curriculum areas. The proposed documentation is easy to adapt and provides a simple example of how such integrated work can be built into a whole-school framework for each of the distinct curriculum areas.

Appendices

You will find here brief descriptions of the games used in the lesson plans and of the drama strategies or conventions that are highlighted in them (indicated in bold when these elements are referred to in the text). This is followed by some recommended story-books that you might like to use to plan your own dramas; and some books and articles on the practice of drama that you might find useful.

How to use this book

If you are relatively inexperienced in teaching drama. The lesson plans are designed to offer as much clarity and advice as possible to enable you to have a go at teaching them as they stand. However, you may well wish to select certain activities that you feel more comfortable with in order to build up your confidence. The activities are therefore separated and numbered to help you adapt the plans in any way that you wish. This section of the book should be of most immediate interest to you but the remaining chapters should help you better understand the intent and purpose behind much of the work.

If you are more experienced in teaching drama. In this case, there is likely to be much in the lessons that you are already familiar with. You will doubtless cast a critical eye over Chapter 1 and be more confident in choosing either to teach the lessons as they stand or to adapt them to suit your own ideas. You may well decide that your own drama lessons are much better! Either way, you may wish to move quickly on to Chapter 2 which could help you plan your own drama lessons with an enhanced understanding of where and how they can relate to a social and moral curriculum.

If you have subject responsibility for drama. It is hoped that Chapter 2 will enhance your ability to argue for drama's importance within the school community; and Chapter 3 is intended to help you draw up the necessary documentation to plan for and monitor its teaching throughout the school.

Chapter 1
Schemes of work

Year 1
Traditional tales and fairy stories: The Frog Prince

Sources:

For the oral telling: *The Classic Fairy Tales*, Maria Tatar (ed.), 1999, Norton Critical Editions, London and New York.
For the sequel: *The Frog Prince Continued* by John Scieszka, 1991, Viking, London

National Literacy Strategy: Year 1 Term 2

Word Level Work
Word recognition
W5
Text Level Work
Fiction and Poetry
● Reading comprehension
  T4; T5; T6; T7; T8; T9; T10
● Writing composition
  T14; T15; T16
Non-fiction
● Writing composition
  T25

Social and Moral Themes

Friendship
● choosing friends
● loneliness, being without friends
Property and Power
● the value of property
Respecting Differences
● respect and concern for others
● empathy for those in different
  circumstances

The story

The Frog Prince is one of the more famous of Grimm's fairy tales and can be said to belong to the 'Animal Groom' cycle of stories, where a girl takes an animal as a husband, often to find out that he is really a handsome prince under some kind of spell. *Beauty and the Beast* is the most famous western example of such a tale. In the original version of the story, the princess's father insists that she keep her promise to the frog, to let him eat off her plate and sleep on her bed, for having retrieved her golden ball when it fell into a well. Once in her bedroom, however, the princess throws the frog against the wall in disgust and, as he hits it, he transforms into a prince whom she marries the following day. In many versions for young children, these sexual and violent connotations are softened into the princess being called upon to give the frog a kiss, with the kiss itself bringing about his transformation. The beauty of presenting an oral version of the tale is that you can use whichever version you like and make other adaptations. I choose to present the oral retelling as faithfully as possible to the original Grimms' tale. In this way children are presented with an alternative to the version we use in the ensuing drama.

Why this story?

- Like other classic fairy tales, it provides children with structural patterns and motifs that reoccur in many stories – forests where young girls venture and where magic happens; animals that can talk or that transform into humans; spells that need to be broken. By becoming aware of such motifs, children can learn the essential building blocks to help them create their own stories.
- Fairy tales are often symbolically about growing up and the dangers or challenges that lie in wait in the outside world (e.g. *The Three Little Pigs, Little Red Riding Hood, The Gingerbread Man*). Some educationalists worry about the reactionary moral values they contain – that happiness for a young girl is defined in terms of marrying into money, for example, and for a boy in terms of showing courage. Others are concerned about the violence of their imagery – the gingerbread man, Red Riding Hood and two of the little pigs are all eaten. There is not enough room here to debate these issues. However, the violence in many of these tales is symbolic rather than realistic and is almost always playful; and there are differing and updated versions of many of the tales that children can enjoy and appreciate *only if they know the originals*. At the end of this particular project, I strongly recommend that you read the sequel by John Scieszka (see above for details).

The drama

The drama lessons below are between 30 to 40 minutes in length and can be taught in the hall or in any large, clear space. The plans are followed by a short section suggesting further drama activities with traditional tales and how you can incorporate them into your classroom.

Why this drama?

- It is very simple and allows children first and foremost to dwell within the story world, to explore it and get to know it better.
- It explores some simple moral issues, mainly relating to the situation of the frog prince and the princess's reluctance to help him.
- It offers a simple introduction to working in role for both children and teacher, assisted by the use of a glove puppet. (Such puppets can be made or purchased. The one I used was ordered from Folkmanis Inc., Emeryville, California, 94608, USA. These puppets are very well made and extremely good value.)

Story: The Frog Prince
LESSON ONE

Key moral ideas
- Property and values

Key learning objectives in drama
By the end of the lesson, children will have:
- become well acquainted with the story of *The Frog Prince*
- had the chance to demonstrate and/or watch some simple mime

Resources
Walking stick; golden ball; small box

Sequence of Activities
1. As a warm-up, adapt the game *Knights, Dogs and Trees* into the game *Frogs, Princesses and Trees*. Before starting, ask the children for suggestions as to how they might represent each shape.

2. Sit the children down and tell the tale of *The Frog Prince*. You can make the telling that much more dramatic by individualising the voices of the characters (petulant for the princess, croaky for the frog); adding facial expression (e.g. disgust from the princess as the frog eats her food); using gesture (e.g. miming the princess gingerly picking up the frog; having your hand physicalise the frog jumping across the floor and on to the table); using a simple prop such as the golden ball; and by varying the pace and dynamic of the telling (e.g. a slight gasp and a pause when the princess realises that her ball has disappeared down the well).

3. Organise the children into a circle and have them act out the tale as you tell it. Use something such as an old walking stick as a **story wand** that, with the children's help, will conjure up the story inside the circle. Explain that you will retell the tale and that children can volunteer to become the characters in the circle. You will tell them exactly what to do, what to say and how to say it. Use the story wand to point to volunteers and every so often wave it through the air to clear the circle and allow new volunteers to continue.

4. Still in the circle, ask the children why they think the golden ball might be so special to the princess, more than her pearls or her crown. Ask them to think of something special to them, without telling what it is. Then place a box in the centre of the circle and **mime** taking out an imaginary golden ball, throwing it in the air, bouncing it, etc. Ask the children what it was

and how they could tell it was a ball. Then ask for volunteers to come into the centre and pretend to take their special thing out of the box. Tell them it doesn't matter if it wouldn't fit into the box in real life. Once they have taken it out, we have to watch what they do with it and try to work out what it is.

Assessment criteria
Do the children listen to the story?
Do they join in with acting it out?
How well do they mime their special things?
How well do they observe the mimes of others?

Discussion/circle time

1. Ask the children to talk about the things they treasure most. Perhaps they can bring something in to show to the class and explain why it means a lot to them. Encourage them to consider the different reasons why we value certain possessions beyond their monetary worth.

2. Tell the children a story of when you lost or accidentally damaged something you treasured. Ask the children to share similar personal stories. What happened afterwards? What would they like to have happened?

Story: The Frog Prince
LESSON TWO

Key moral ideas
● Loneliness
● Respect and concern for others

Key learning objectives in drama
By the end of the lesson, children will have:
● helped represent and sequence events from the story
● joined in with some sustained imaginative role play to help create a new part of the tale
● responded in role to a puppet/teacher in role

Resources
Puppet; story wand; ring-binder disguised as a book of spells

Sequence of Activities

1. Sit the children in a circle and tell them you are going to show them half of a picture taken from the story of *The Frog Prince*. Then freeze into a character from the story at a part when you are evidently engaged in some action with another character, e.g. as the princess looking down in disgust at the frog as she opens the door to him. Ask children who they think the character was and what part of the story you were illustrating. Then ask for volunteers who think they can complete the image by freezing as the other character missing from the picture. A few possibilities can be tried and children can be asked to comment on what they see. A child can also be asked to copy and take on your character. Do three or four of these, illustrating different parts of the story, then ask children if they can sequence the pictures in the order they would appear in a book, i.e. chronologically.

2. Ask the children why they think the witch might have turned the prince into a frog. Listen to their different ideas and use as many of them as possible to invent a short, improvised telling of what really happened. **Narrate** this with the **story wand** and have children volunteer to act it out. Use the children in the circle to help you with the narration by, for example, asking them for advice as to what the witch, the prince and any other characters they include might have said at different points.

3. Praise the children for making up this missing part of the story and tell them that you want them to imagine that they are in the forest where the frog prince lives, long before the princess set him free and before anyone

knew that would happen. Let the children move around the space, exploring the forest, and provide some narration to help them.

4. Introduce the frog puppet, sit the children down and tell them (**teacher in role** as the frog) how you used to be a prince and relate the story enacted in Activity 2 to explain how and why you were turned into a frog. Ask the children if they can imagine what it is like to live alone in the forest, with no friends and no family. Talk about this and then ask them if they would help you find out how to be set free. Lead them through the wood in search of the witch's cottage. Point to it in a space and ask children if they can see it too. Ask individual volunteers to describe it – is it made of gingerbread? Is it very big or very small? Tell them that you are too small to see through the window – what do they think the witch might be doing inside? How can the children find out without letting her know we're all here? Very quietly creep up to the window and peep in.

5. Take off the puppet, sit the children down and choose a volunteer to be sculpted into the witch, stirring her cauldron perhaps, or whatever the children think. Is she a very evil witch? If so, ask the children to help make the sculpture look as evil as possible. Encourage other children to demonstrate how she might look.

6. Tell the children that, in order to help the frog, they will need to take the witch's book of spells from her. Sit them in a circle and play a version of the game *Keeper of the Keys*, with a child blindfolded as the witch in the centre of the circle. Instead of a set of keys have a large ring-binder with 'Book of Spells' written on the cover. Play this three or four times and at least until the book of spells is successfully taken.

7. End the session on a note of anticipation. I wonder if there is a spell in the book that will tell the frog how he can be set free. . .?

Assessment criteria
Can children complete and sequence the images in Activity 1?
How imaginative and relevant are the ideas the children provide in Activity 2?
How readily do the children engage with the fictional world in Activities 3 and 5?
How well do they join in with the role play/teacher in role in Activity 4?

Discussion/circle time

1. Can children share stories of a time when they were lost or felt lonely, like the frog prince? Did anyone help them? How?
2. Have they ever helped anyone in trouble or who was lonely or unhappy? A new pupil at the school, perhaps? Did that make them feel better?

Story: The Frog Prince
LESSON THREE

Key moral ideas
- Empathy for those in different circumstances
- Respect and concern for others

Key learning objectives in drama
By the end of the lesson, children will have:
- engaged in sustained role play
- used language to persuade
- demonstrated physical, expressive control

Resources
Frog puppet; book of spells; golden ball; tambourine

Sequence of Activities

1. Play the game *I walked through the forest and I saw a. . .* This is adapted from *I went to the market*, with each child in turn naming a different animal they met in the wood. It can also be used to reinforce the alphabet if children are asked to name the animals in alphabetical order – an ant, a bear, a cat, a dog, an elephant, etc. You can prompt by helping the whole class sound out the letters in turn 'I walked through the wood and I saw a gggg. . .'

2. Recap with the children what has happened so far in our story and bring out the book of spells. Open it carefully and show some surprise at finding a spell inside, written in large writing (which, of course, you had prepared earlier!). Have a child or two volunteer to read it aloud and then have the whole class read it together. Ask them what they think it means. It is best if the spell can be written in simple verse, something like:
   If Frog you are and prince would be
   A fair princess you first must see.
   Become her friend, for only she
   With her kiss can set you free.

3. Put on the puppet and, as the frog, explain sadly that you are sure the princess would never kiss you, because you're so ugly and she is so proud. Have any of the children met the princess? What is she like? Do they think they could persuade her? Could they try to be polite, otherwise she might not listen to them.

4. Have the children help you set up the room in the castle where the princess will see them. Will there be a throne? Where shall we have it? How will she look as she sits on it? Will she be playing with anything? The golden ball, perhaps? Then, as **teacher in role** as the princess, be awkward and difficult and make the children work hard to persuade you to kiss the frog. Eventually, send a child to fetch the frog puppet and, with either yourself or a child wearing it, pull a face and say that the children will have to show you how. Let some children volunteer to kiss the frog and ask them each time what it was like – was it really horrible? In the end make a big show of kissing the frog.

5. Ask the children to find a space in which they will show how the frog turned into the prince. First they make a frog shape, then a prince shape. Let the children view four or five of these and discuss what they like about them. Encourage them to copy one another's ideas. Then, using a tambourine to guide the transition, have the children **perform** the transformation altogether. These can be viewed by having six or so individuals perform them at once.

Assessment criteria
How well do the children sustain the role play in Activities 3 and 4?
What sort of reasons do they use when trying to persuade the princess to kiss the frog?
How controlled and physically expressive are they in Activity 5?

Discussion/circle time

1. What do they think of the princess's attitude before she kissed the frog? Is she the kind of person they would like as a friend? Why/why not?
2. What kind of things did she say about the frog? Were they fair? Why/why not? How do they think the frog prince must have felt listening to her saying those things about him?
3. Play the **game** *What do we like about. . .?*

Other drama activities for work with traditional tales

Finger puppet theatre

Figure 1.1 illustrates a simple and quick way for children to make finger puppets so that they can retell the story with dialogue, either on their own, with a partner or in small groups. Children in Year 1 will need some initial help in small groups but, once they catch on to the method, they will enjoy making them on their own. It will help greatly if, as an introduction to this work, you make your own puppets first and retell a section of the story using them yourself, perhaps during a plenary section of the literacy hour.

Step 1

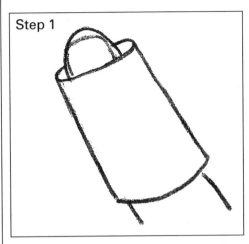

Cut out a strip of paper, measure it around your finger and glue into a cylinder shape.

Step 2

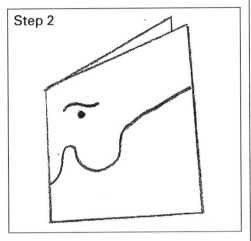

Fold in half a strip of paper to create face. Cut out profile and include tabs at the rear.

Step 3

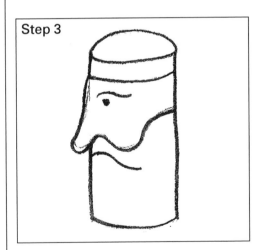

Glue to the cylinder creating a 3D effect by protruding nose and cheeks. Using different coloured paper enhances the effect.

Step 4

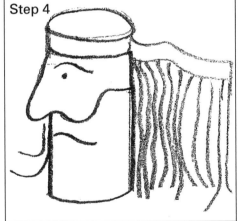

Cut out strip of paper for hair. Cut this into narrow strips leaving a small, uncut margin at the top. Curl the hair by pulling over the blade of the scissors. You can add a hat or crown (see Figure 1.2).

Figure 1.1 Making a finger puppet

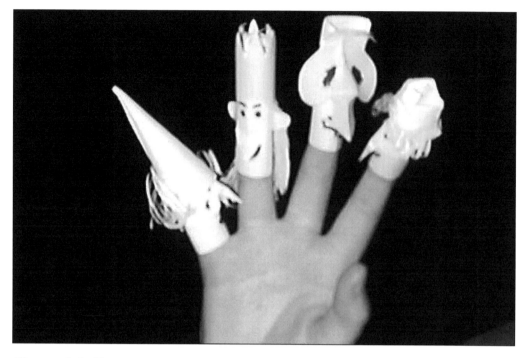

Figure 1.2 Finger puppets

The imaginative play area

A fairy tale kitchen/dining room is easy to create in the imaginative play area. For *The Frog Prince*, a table with 'silver' plates and beakers will suffice to begin with. The particular identity of the room could change as you focus on different tales by altering certain props or aspects of the 'set'. For example:

- Three different sized chairs and bowls for *The Three Bears*.
- A mixing bowl, plastic rolling pin, flour tin and biscuit box on the table for *The Gingerbread Man*.
- Grandma's knitting, knitting patterns, and a 'Happy Birthday Grandma' card for her cottage in *Little Red Riding Hood*.
- In the case of the ogre's kitchen in *Jack and the Beanstalk*, children could be encouraged to imagine its giant size by role playing with their finger puppets in the area.

You might also have a large picture stuck to the wall representing the view from the window. This, too, could change from tale to tale to show the frog prince hopping up the castle steps; a cow and a farmer chasing a gingerbread man; and the wolf walking up the path for *Red Riding Hood* or *The Three Little Pigs*.

A number of activities within the imaginative play area can be framed to include both literacy and moral issues. If you organise your class so that they do a carousel of group activities over the week in the literacy hour, then work in the imaginative play area can be included in your literacy planning. In this way, every group would have a 20-minute session in the play area once a week. If these groups are set according to ability, then the activity could remain the same but the written/reading materials could be differentiated from day to day. Such activities will normally benefit from a short input of a minute or two from the **teacher in role** before they begin. Examples might include:

- *The Frog Prince.* The princess and the prince are on their honeymoon and can't do the shopping. Can the children look in their cupboards and make a shopping list for the week?
- *The Three Little Pigs.* Mrs Pig has received a letter from one of her children but she has mislaid her glasses. Can the children read it for her? It informs her that he feels very safe in his house of straw. She becomes very worried as she knows what the Big Bad Wolf can do. Can the children write a reply to him, warning him of the danger and giving him advice?
- *Red Riding Hood.* Grandmother needs her eyes testing. Children take on the roles of optician and grandmother and test whether she can read a selection of cards and charts that you have prepared. These should reinforce words and phonics being studied in the literacy hour.
- *The Three Bears.* The Bear Family have found that lots of things seem to be broken since Goldilocks' visit, as well as Baby Bear's chair. They have called in some workers (the children) to find out exactly what needs fixing. Can they examine the windows, kitchen fittings, etc., and make a list of the jobs that need doing?

Literacy objectives and related activities.

Pupils should be taught: **Fiction and Poetry**	*Examples from this chapter*
Reading comprehension 4. to retell stories, giving the main points in sequence and to notice differences between written and spoken forms in retelling, e.g. by comparing oral versions with the written text; to refer to relevant phrases and sentences;	*Children sequence the images from the tale of* The Frog Prince *at the start of Lesson 2.* *They compare your oral version with other versions.*
5. to identify and record some key features of story language from a range of stories, and to practise reading and using them, e.g. in oral retellings;	*The children perform their own retellings with finger puppets.*

6. to identify and discuss a range of story themes, and to collect and compare;	*Begin building a class chart of all the traditional tales you work with this term. Include where the stories take place; the good characters; the bad characters; and how the stories end.*
7. to discuss reasons for, or causes of, incidents in stories;	*The children speculate upon how and why the witch turned the prince into a frog (Lesson 2).* *The children tell the princess why she must kiss the frog (Lesson 3).*
8. to identify and discuss characters, e.g. appearance, behaviour, qualities; to speculate about how they might behave; to discuss how they are described in the text; and to compare characters from different stories or plays;	*In Lesson 3 and in circle time the children discuss the character of the princess. They compare her to other girls in fairy tales, e.g. Goldilocks. They compare the witch in their story with other fairy tale witches.*
9. to become aware of character and dialogue, e.g. by role-playing parts when reading aloud stories or plays with others;	*Script small scenes for the children to perform as a puppet theatre.*
10. to identify and compare basic story elements, e.g. beginnings and endings in different stories;	*Children compare the beginning and ending of the tale with John Scieszka's* The Frog Prince Continued.
Writing composition 14. to represent outlines of story plots using captions, pictures, arrows, etc., to record main incidents in order to make, for example, a class book, wall story, own version;	*Children in groups make a pictorial* ***'map' of the story***. *These are used to inform a class wall display, where characters, places and incidents in the story are illustrated and written about by the children.*
15. to build simple profiles of characters from stories read, describing characteristics, appearances, behaviour with pictures, single words, captions, words and sentences from text;	*Children draw pictures and write short descriptions of the frog prince and the princess.*

16. to use some of the elements of known stories to structure own writing;	*Children draw a picture and write about the part of the story it illustrates.*
Non-fiction: writing composition 25. to assemble information from own experience . . . to write simple, non-chronological reports; and to organise in lists, separate pages, charts;	*The lists children write for prince and princess and for Mr and Mrs Bear in the play area.*
Word Level Work: word recognition 5. to read on sight familiar words, e.g. children's names, equipment labels, classroom captions;	*Children read these words in the play corner, in role as grandmother and doctor, while role playing the eye test.*

Year 2
Tinker Jim

Source:

Tinker Jim by Gillian Maclure and Paul Coltman, 1992, Scholastic Children's Books, London.

National Literacy Strategy: Year 2 Term 2	**Social and Moral Themes**
Text Level Work Fiction and Poetry ● Reading comprehension **T4; T6; T7; T8; T9; T10** ● Writing composition **T13; T14; T15**	*Rules* ● law breaking and wrongdoing ● justice and fairness *Property and Power* ● sharing and not sharing ● stealing ● punishment ● the consequences of crime *Respecting Differences* ● respect and concern for others ● empathy for those in different circumstances

The story

Tinker Jim is a narrative poem accompanied by detailed, colourful illustrations that provide additional information to inform the narrative. The early stanzas establish the pattern of the verse and set the tone of the tale:

> *Tinker Jim was very thin.*
> *He found his food where he could.*
> *And when his pot had nothing in,*
> *He went on the prowl*
> *For a duck or a fowl*
> *And cooked them alone in the wood.*

Tinker Jim lives in a wood in an old chicken house near the village of Cudeleigh. He is old now, and also rather lazy, and doesn't enjoy the kind of food that can be easily come by in the wood – baked hedgehog, nettle soup and the like. On hearing that the local vicar, the Reverend Obadiah Delves, will give out food 'to those less fortunate than ourselves', Jim thinks 'That's me!' However, on visiting the rectory, he is only offered cat food so he turns his attention to neighbouring Cudeleigh Towers, the home of Lady Millicent Mulberry Higg. She is plump and obviously well fed and Jim spies her butler leaving her garage with enormous plates of appetising food. That night, he breaks into the garage and finds a large freezer packed full of expensive food and he steals some, returning regularly on successive nights for more. Over time Jim becomes selective in what he takes and also begins to smarten up his chicken house. Looking at himself in a mirror, he realises how dirty and shabby he looks, so he washes himself in the river, trims his beard and steals some smart clothes from the washing line at Cudeleigh Towers. This proves to be his downfall, however. Next day, as he strolls all trim and proper into town, his smart clothes arouse the suspicions of a policeman. He is arrested and spends six months in prison. On leaving prison, Jim returns to his old style of life. We are informed that he is 'thinner and had learned a bit more' and we leave him cooking a rabbit for his dinner.

Why this story?

- It is an engaging, humorous tale and the illustrations provide many delightful and witty additional details that embellish the narrative at the same time as they draw children into the fictional world.
- Jim is a likeable rogue, the kind of mischievous, comical outsider whose adventures children enjoy.
- Although children know that Jim's stealing is wrong, there is an underlying ambiguity to the morality of the story inasmuch as he himself is wronged by the vicar, who should represent the moral order. It is a delightfully subversive tale.
- The narrative line of the poem is clear but some aspects of it, in particular its complex rhyme pattern, will reward detailed attention.

The drama

The drama described below closely follows the narrative of the story outlined above. It is intended to be taught before the children are introduced to the book, before they even know that there is a book. It is best taught in a large space such as the hall but can be adapted for the classroom. I have presented it in three sessions, each of which should take between 50 to 60 minutes. Although there are a lot of activities in each session, the pace should be kept brisk and active.

Why this drama?

- By helping children live the story and know the principal characters, it should create a strong desire to explore the text when it is presented to them.
- It is designed to encourage them to articulate their own sense of social justice and injustice and to help them explore their ideas of charity, generosity, selfishness and greed.
- The characters are essentially comic so, consequently, the drama is a lot of fun, for children and teacher. It is a good example of how exploring moral issues need not be pious!

Proposed timescale for work: 3–4 weeks

You may only be able to teach one drama session per week owing to limited access to the hall space. However, if possible, it is best to teach the drama sessions over two rather than three weeks, thus providing a more concentrated experience of the story. You may well be able to complete the literacy activities listed at the end of this section within the same week but the scheme below makes allowance for additional English time in the subsequent week should you need it.

Week 1	Week 2	Week 3	Week 4
Drama: Session 1 *Additional English time*	Drama: Sessions 2 and 3 *Additional English time*	The book Discussion and written tasks *Literacy hour Circle time Additional English time (if needed)*	Discussion and written tasks *Literacy hour Additional English time (if needed)*

Story: Tinker Jim
LESSON ONE

Key moral ideas
- Sharing/not sharing
- Respect and concern for others

Key learning objectives in drama
By the end of the lesson, children will have:
- considered how costume and objects suggest character
- actively participated in role throughout the lesson
- identified with the characters and actions of Jim and the vicar

Resources
Create Jim's clearing in a corner of the space. Place in it the following items of costume: a scarf, flat cap, old jacket and a walking stick. Also place in it an old tin cooking pot and a basket beside a chair. A prepared poster (*see 5 below*) and tin of cat food should be hidden in the basket.

Sequence of Activities
1. Inform the children that you and they are going to work on a story together and that a lot of this story will take place in a wood. Using the whole of the space, the children creep as if through the wood. They practise moving and freezing in silence.
2. Sit on the chair and tell the children that this is a clearing in Cudeleigh Wood and that they are the children from the nearby Cudeleigh village. They have heard rumours of a stranger who has recently started living in this clearing. Their aim is to get to the bushes that surround the clearing and to hide behind them. Successively covering and uncovering your eyes, play a version of **grandmother's footsteps** until all the children are quietly seated around Jim's space.
3. Introduce the costume and possessions within the clearing. Encourage the children to speculate on the man who owns them – whether he is young or old, rich or poor, etc. – and on what questions they might ask him if they could talk to him.
4. Put on the items of costume – **narrate** your way into the character (**teacher in role**). 'Tinker Jim was old and thin. He'd spent his life moving from place to place, always living out of doors and now he was seated outside of the tiny shed where he slept, in a clearing in Cudeleigh wood.' Then notice the children and talk to them freely. You need to establish:
   - that Jim is friendly and can be trusted (by offering to treat a child's wart, for example);
   - something of his history, as detailed in the book;

- his laziness and his inability to catch his own food any more – also his dislike of delicacies such as baked hedgehog and coots' eggs. Hence his hunger.

5. When you judge it appropriate, show the children the poster you collected from outside of Cudeleigh Rectory, where the vicar lives. You are short-sighted and have lost your glasses. Have the children help you read it. The poster can be written with your class in mind – below is an example you may wish to adopt:

   The Reverend and Mrs Obadiah Delves
   Of Cudeleigh Rectory
   To those less fortunate than themselves
   Will give out food for free.
   If you would taste what's on their shelves
   Be there by half past three.

6. In haste, ask for a child who knows the way to the rectory to lead the way there, not forgetting to take your bag with you. Once there, quietly creep up to the window and comment on all the lovely food you can see spread on the table. Invite individual children to look through the window and ask them to describe in detail what they can see there.

7. Ask the children to hide and keep quiet while you knock on the door. Promise them you will share with them any food you are given. Tell them you can hear the vicar coming to the door, doff your cap and talk to him. (Perform this like a telephone conversation – the children only hear what Jim says). Accept his invitation into the rectory with a wink to the children, freeze and come out of role. Ask the children to imagine what Jim will leave the house with. Ask for volunteers to **model** different versions of how he will look and what he might say when he leaves the house.

8. Resume the drama **in role** as Jim. Look disappointed and confused and slowly pull a tin of cat food out of your bag. Still in role, discuss the vicar's 'generosity' and what the children think of it. What should Jim have done? Refuse the cat food? Make the vicar feel ashamed of himself? What should he have said to convince the vicar that he was wrong? Trial this as **forum theatre**, with Jim pretending to be the vicar while a child takes on the role of Jim (wearing his cap).

9. After you have solicited comments and opinions, have the children help Jim write a letter to the vicar to try and make him feel ashamed of his actions.

Assessment criteria

Can children make appropriate suggestions about Jim's character from the objects in the clearing?

Do they sustain their roles and participate appropriately?

How effectively do they model Jim's and the vicar's responses in Activities 7 and 8?

What kind of objections do they offer to the vicar's behaviour and how are these expressed in the letter?

Story: Tinker Jim
LESSON TWO

Key moral ideas
- The value of property
- Concern for others
- Sharing/not sharing

Key learning objectives in drama
By the end of the lesson, children will have:
- sustained roles in whole class and small group drama
- demonstrated some simple activities through mime
- shown an ability to improvise dramatic play where different views are expressed

Resources
As with Lesson One. Also a reply from the vicar. A lavish hat for Lady Higg.

Sequence of Activities
1. Play a tag game 'Tinker Jim chasing the chickens'. Whichever child is wearing Jim's hat is 'it'. Switch the hat to a different child every so often.
2. Recap the work from last session. Before resuming the drama, inform the children that they must be prepared for you to play a new character in the story, as well as Tinker Jim.
3. In the clearing, **in role** as Jim, sit with the reply from the vicar's letter. This should be written on two, large sheets of paper so the children can read it with you.

> Dear Tinker Jim,
>   I am sorry you did not appreciate my generous gift. My wife thinks you should learn to look after yourself so she has written out a recipe for nettle soup.
> Yours sincerely,
> Reverend Obadiah Delves.

> *NETTLE SOUP*
> You need:
>   One onion
>   One potato
>   The tips of a hundred nettles
>   Water

1. First chop up the onion and put it in the pot.
2. Then chop up the potato and put it in the pot.
3. Next chop up the nettles and put them in the pot.
4. Add the water and let it boil.

5. First read out the letter with the children's help, then read it through together. Do the same with the menu, allowing some time for comment.
6. Organise the children to help you make nettle soup. Ask them to collect the nettle tips for you. Perhaps you have some old gloves you can **mime** handing to them! Some children can mime the other activities for you. When everything is in the pot it can cook very quickly! Then react with suitable disgust to the taste and let those children who wish to do the same.
7. Jim wonders about the lady who lives in Cudeleigh Towers. He has seen her and she looks rich and well fed. Her name is Lady Millicent Mulberry Higg. Perhaps she'll have some food to spare for him? Jim is too discouraged to go and ask for himself after what happened at the rectory? Will the children go and plead on his behalf? Jim insists that they must be polite and rehearses with them the kind of things they will say to the lady.
8. The way through the wood to Cudeleigh Towers is very winding. Play a follow the leader-style game to get there.
9. Out of role, sit the children down in a circle. Tell them they are about to meet Lady Higg but before that they will have a chance to watch her alone in her garden. Ask them to look out for the things she likes and thinks are important. **In role** as Lady Higg, wander about your garden and talk about how you love your flowers, trees, house, gate, car(s), jewellery, etc., because they're the biggest and most expensive in Cudeleigh. Come out of role and ask the children what they have learned about her so far.
10. **In role** as Lady Higg, tell the children you will invite two of them for tea, the ones with the nicest manners. If they have anything special to talk to you about, they can do it then. Teach the children how to drink tea properly (with their little finger stuck out straight!) and how to say 'kindly pass the crumpets, vicar'. Do this as an exaggerated parody. Explain that you are expecting the vicar and his wife for tea.
11. Put the children into groups of three. One is to be Lady Higg, the other two the children of the village whom Lady Higg has invited to take tea. Remind the children of the purpose of their visit – to plead for food on Tinker Jim's behalf. Let the groups **act out** the outcome through improvisation. After a very few minutes, stop the groups and ask each group whether Lady Higg has agreed to help Jim or not. Briefly discuss the reasons for their decision with each group.

12. It is more than likely that many groups will have Lady Higg agree to help Jim. Sit the children in a circle and choose one such group. Improvise a scene with them where you arrive **in role** as the vicar or the vicar's wife. On hearing of Lady Higg's decision to help Tinker Jim, inform her of his ingratitude to your generous gift and try to convince her to change her mind.

13. Out of role, ask the children what food they have managed to get for Tinker Jim. Ask for volunteers to show how they think he will look when he sees the food.

Assessment criteria

How well can the children sustain their roles, particularly in Activity 11?

How well do the children execute the simple mime activities?

How well do the children in Activity 12 argue against the vicar/vicar's wife?

Story: Tinker Jim
LESSON THREE

Key moral ideas
- Stealing
- Crime and punishment

Learning objectives in drama
By the end of the lesson, children will have:
- extended their mime skills
- expressed in role the attitudes that the different characters in the story might hold towards Jim

Resources
Usual items of costume
Skipping rope, 'smart' jacket and scarf pegged to it to make a washing line
Two cut-out paper sacks, marker pen
Large sheet prepared to represent the front page of the local paper (see Activity 5)

Sequence of Activities
1. Ask children for suggestions as to their favourite food. Write them on the prepared sacks. Read what's in each sack together.
2. Sit the children in a circle and place the sacks in the centre. Explain that the space within it represents Lady Higg's garage. Explain that Jim enjoyed the food so much that he went back for more and, when chased by the butler, thought he'd help himself anyway. Play a version of the game *The Farmer and the Fox* to see if Jim can escape with a sack of food. One child volunteers to be Jim and leaves the circle, standing with his/her eyes closed, facing the wall. Select someone to be the butler in the circle by touching them on the shoulder. The butler can't chase Jim until he's picked up the sack. If he tags him before he leaves the circle then he's caught. Jim can only leave the circle at the same place he entered it. Play it three or four times, changing the children each time.
3. Have a smart jacket and scarf pegged to a skipping rope. Ask two children to hold it in the centre of the circle and have another child dress in Jim's costume. **Narrate** a short introduction and tell Jim to **mime** the actions as you narrate them. '*One evening, as Jim was leaving yet again with some food, he caught sight of some smart clothes on the line. He looked at them closely – they looked clean; he touched the jacket – it felt soft; he felt his own jacket and pulled a face – urgghh! It felt. . .*' Ask the children how they think it felt. Involve them in the narration of the scene in this way, asking them to suggest the actions for Jim to mime. They will almost invariably

suggest that he steals the jacket and scarf and may well have him leave his own on the line in their place!

4. Briefly discuss what the children think of Jim's actions, stealing the food and then the clothes. Do they think he'll be caught?

5. Show them the prepared headline of the 'Cudeleigh News'. *Thief Caught at Cudeleigh Towers – Tinker Jim held at Police Station*. Ask if any children would like to demonstrate how they think Jim might look in the photo on the front page. Have a child take on the role of Jim in the police station. Encourage the class to read his emotions and thoughts. Then **hot seat** one of the children in role as Jim to find out how exactly he was caught.

6. In small groups, determined by the story created in the previous exercise, children **mime** how Jim was captured. Provide the narration to this in order to help them structure and pace the action. (Alternatively, let children **act out** the scene independently.)

7. Ask the children if they know what happens when people get caught committing crimes. Stage a **meeting** in the form of a magistrate's hearing. Explain that witnesses can be questioned to either speak for or against Jim and that Jim can speak himself. Ask the children who in the story might say helpful things about Jim and who might say unhelpful things. Children can volunteer to take on these roles when the magistrate calls for them. Insist that no one should tell lies or make things up in court. **In role** as the magistrate, ask for the different characters to come out and answer your questions one at a time. Small items of costume might help the children here – a hat for Lady Higg, a bible for the vicar, etc. After you have heard people speak both against Jim and on his behalf, explain that Jim is clearly guilty and that the normal punishment is to be sent to prison for six months. You can't just let him off. Have the children any alternative ideas to sending Jim to prison? Conclude by coming out of role and asking the children what they would like the magistrate to decide and what they think he actually will decide.

8. Don't make a decision but let children know that they will find out what happened to Jim when you read them the story. Show them the book now, for the first time!

Assessment criteria

How clearly do children mime the actions in Activities 3 and 6? Do they respond to the tension you create with your narration?

How appropriate are the opinions children express in role in Activity 7 to the characters they are playing and to the events of the story?

How thoughtfully do they discuss the problem of finding a fair punishment for Jim?

Literacy objectives and related activities

Pupils should be taught: **Fiction and Poetry**	***Examples from this chapter***
Reading comprehension 4. to predict story endings/incidents;	*The children are often asked throughout the drama to predict what they think will happen next; how Jim will look when he leaves the rectory; what he will do when he sees the clothes on the line, etc.*
6. to identify and describe characters, expressing own views and using words and phrases from texts;	*Children are asked to describe and give their opinions about Jim, the vicar, Lady Higg, during the drama and to back this up with references to what they did/said*
7. to prepare and retell stories individually and through role play in groups, using dialogue and narrative from text;	*The drama sessions meet this objective and, within them, children prepare and enact sections of the story.*
8. to read own poems aloud;	*See T15, below.*
9. to identify and discuss patterns of rhythm, rhyme and other features of sound in different poems;	*Children compare these features of the verse structure of Tinker Jim with, for example, that of the standard limerick.*
10. to comment on and recognise when the reading aloud of a poem makes sense and is effective;	*Children look at how the punctuation of the poem helps indicate when the reader should or should not pause at the end of a line. The teacher models some examples of good/bad reading for the children to comment on.*

Writing composition	
13. to use story settings from reading, e.g. redescribe, use in own writing;	*Children draw a map of Cudeleigh and its surroundings and describe what can be found there.*
14. to write character profiles, e.g. simple descriptions, posters, passports, using key words and phrases that describe or are spoken by characters in the text;	*Tinker Jim's prison file or a 'Wanted' poster; Lady Higg's passport; a description of the vicar in the parish newsletter.* *As a class, list examples of good and bad ethical action as shown by Jim and/or Lady Higg, referring to examples from the book and the drama.*
15. to use structures from poems as a basis for writing by . . . inventing own lines/verses;	*Children write a missing verse for the book, describing how Tinker Jim obtains food near the beginning of the book, or his time in prison near the end. The illustrations provide the necessary details.*

Discussion/circle time

Much of the moral discussion takes place within the drama but the following topics could be talked about in class after the children have listened to the story.

1. Who are the characters that share in the story? Which of them doesn't share? Do children like their friends to share with them? What kind of things? Do they always share their sweets and their toys? When do they/don't they? What does it feel like when someone *won't* share with you?
2. Divide children into groups of four or five. Give a different number of biscuits to each group – two to one group, six or seven to another. Then tell them they can all eat a biscuit. Some groups will not have enough to go round so ask them what can be done about this. Then ask if they think it is fair for those who have more than they need to share with those who don't have enough.
3. The vicar's behaviour is obviously not what the children expect. How should a religious minister behave? Why? What do the children understand by the terms 'charity' and 'charitable'? Do they know of any charitable organisations? What do they know about the work, for example, of 'Children in Need' or 'Comic Relief'? Can they think of anything that the school does to help people who need help?
4. Jim has to live in the open. Is it comfortable? Will it be comfortable in winter? What about when it rains?

5. In the book, we see Jim very hungry, and, later, very ill, having eaten too much rich food from Lady Higg's freezer. Perhaps children can share some stories about when they have been very hungry and when they have made themselves ill by eating too much!

6. What do the children think of Jim's punishment? Do they think it was fair? If not, what do they think would have been a fair punishment for him?

7. Encourage the children to share stories about times when they did something to make amends for a wrongdoing. How did this make them/the other person feel?

Year 3
Sho and the Demons of the Deep

Source:

Sho and the Demons of the Deep, written and illustrated by Annouchka Gravel Galouchko, 1998, Annick Press (U.S.) Ltd.

National Literacy Strategy: Year 3 Term 2	Social and Moral Themes
Text Level Work	*Rules*
Fiction and Poetry	● laws and rules
● Reading comprehension	● law breaking and wrongdoing
T2; T3; T4; T5	*Property and Power*
● Writing composition	● the consequences of crime
T7; T8; T10	● the qualities of leadership
Non-fiction	*Community and Environment*
● Reading comprehension	● working together
T12; T14	● responsibility for the environment
Word Level Work	● group and individual
W24	responsibilities

The story

The tale is set in Ancient Japan and is richly and colourfully illustrated in a style reminiscent of traditional Japanese painting. It tells of a time when people were too shy to reveal their secret dreams and so packed their nightmares into bags and threw them into the sea. Here, however, the dreams escape and, as so many demons, cause the sea to rage and storm and sink the people's fishing boats. The people soon grow hungry and desperate. Then two fishermen hear of a young servant girl called Sho who can look into the hearts of all living things and so they go to her and ask for help. She makes them promise to give a week's catch to the poor and to ensure that no one will ever throw their nightmares into the sea again. She then asks them to row her out into the stormy sea and, with her soothing words and voice, she calms the demons of the deep, melting their fury until they disappear. All is returned to normal and, for a while, life continues in harmony. However, people now have nowhere to dispose of their nightmares which begin to oveflow from their cupboards and closets. A strange, sombre figure arrives calling himself the refuse collector and, for the price of a silver coin per bag, he promises to relieve all the people of their nightmares. The people are grateful for this offer but, on leaving the village, he simply dumps their nightmares once more into the sea, which is soon storming and raging worse than ever. This time, when Sho comes to the shore, she speaks directly to the sea, instructing it to spew the demons back onto the land. In one, gigantic wave, the sea ejects the demons, leaving them as a harmless, green sludge on the beach. The villagers sing and dance for joy and the children ask Sho her secret. She answers by telling them to play with their bad dreams rather than fear them; to toss them into the air rather than into the sea. In response, one young boy draws and paints pictures of his dreams and tosses the pictures into the air. Another villager does the same, attaching his dreams to a light frame of wood and holding it with string as they dance and play in the wind. Soon all the villagers are copying him and the first kites have been created.

Why this story?

- The example of good triumphing over evil being achieved by taming rather than killing the monsters provides a good contrast to many traditional tales, fantasy cartoons and computer games.
- There is a strong use of symbol in the story through which children can be led to consider some important personal and environmental issues, namely, what they should and needn't be afraid of; and how we can help prevent environmental pollution.
- As well as providing a beautifully illustrated text for the literacy hour, the book could be used to stimulate lots of exciting work in art, music and dance to complement this drama scheme.

The drama

Much of the drama work proposed below can be done in the classroom. Only the second lesson, which concentrates on movement, needs a large space. The first two sessions are roughly an hour in length and are designed to explore the rich possibilities the story offers for symbolic representation through voice and movement. The third lesson, as explained in the plan, is best spread over three small sessions of 15 minutes each. The activities here are planned to help children explore some of the moral implications in the tale, particularly relating to our responsibility for the environment and the place of laws and rules to help ensure that people behave responsibly. The drama work does not attempt to exhaust all of the possibilities presented by the story. If you have a special interest in dance, for example, you will, on reading the book, notice far more opportunities for movement work than I have detailed here.

Proposed timescale for the work: 1–2 weeks

As these lessons have been planned to need just one lesson in the hall, you may well decide to make this your text for the literacy hour for a week and do all the drama and a selection of the literacy activities over that week.

After your initial reading of the story, there are a number of questions you might discuss with the children before beginning the drama work, e.g. why do the poor people suffer more than rich people when there is a shortage of food? What does Sho do to help the poor people? What do the children think of this demand of hers, that the fishermen give a week's catch to the poor? What do they think the fishermen might have thought of it? Why?

Story: Sho and the Demons of the Deep
LESSON ONE

Key moral ideas
● How we describe/perceive monstrous behaviour
● How we describe/perceive its opposite
● The qualities of leadership

Learning objectives in drama.
By the end of the lesson, children will have;
● experimented with the expressive potential of their voices
● helped create and perform a piece of performance poetry

Resources
Flip chart and pens; drum; bells; cassette recorder and blank tape

Sequence of Activities
1. Discuss with the class how demons are evil and nasty. What kind of evil and nasty things might they do? List these as verbs, e.g. kill; shout; destroy.
2. Practise chanting words from the list in monstrous ways – shouting, hissing, growling, etc. You can ask children for suggestions and perform some examples for them to copy. Then point to different words on the list and ask children to growl them together; or to shout them together, etc.
3. Discuss how Sho was able to soothe the demons with her voice. What does a soothing voice sound like? Have children read one or two words from the list in a soothing voice, and discuss how the voice might be soothing but the words certainly aren't! Ask children to help you make a second list of words that describe the opposite of such behaviour. Use a different coloured pen for this list.
4. Do the same activities for this list as for the monstrous list, only in soothing voices.
5. Now tell the children that you and they are going to make a poem which the whole class can perform. The first half of the poem shall be spoken by voices representing the demons, the second by voices representing Sho. Write the phrase: *We are massive demons, surging from the deep, soon to destroy tiny fishing boats* and ask the children to select from the monstrous list the words that the demons might now speak. Write between four and six. Underneath, write the phrase (spoken by Sho in the book): *You are little dragons, bubbles on the waves, soon to be burst by the playful winds* and get children to choose appropriate words from the list of opposites. The subsequent poem will now read something like:

> 'We are massive demons, surging from the deep,
> Soon to destroy tiny fishing boats.
> Kill!
> Hurt!
> Smash up!
> Destroy!'
> 'You are little dragons, bubbles on the waves,
> Soon to be burst by the playful winds.
> Cure!
> Be kind!
> Repair!
> Create!'

6. Practise reading it through together and decide jointly how the different words in the list will be spoken. Then divide the class into two halves, one half to be the monsters and the other to be Sho. Use the drum to introduce the demons and the bells to introduce Sho. Practise it once, then record it. Then swap parts and repeat the exercise.

Assessment criteria

How expressively do the children use their voices when reading the words from the lists?

How effective are the performances they record?

Discussion/circle time

1. Do the children think the nightmare demons are happy or unhappy creatures? Why?
2. Does Sho make the demons behave by shouting or by frightening them? How *does* she do it?
3. Do the children ever feel they behave a bit like the demons? When? How does it make them/other people feel?
4. Have they ever been calm and soothing like Sho? With a baby, perhaps? Or a pet? How did that make them feel?
5. Would they prefer their teacher to be like one of the demons or like Sho? Why?

Story: Sho and the Demons of the Deep
LESSON TWO

Key moral ideas
- Working together
- Dealing with our fears

Learning objectives in drama
By the end of the lesson, children will have:
- demonstrated controlled and expressive use of movement to represent the nightmare demons
- used silk cloth to represent a stormy and a calm sea

Resources
Lengths of blue silk cloth; bells; drums

Sequence of Activities
1. Ask children to sit opposite a partner, one as A, the other as B. A is to pull different demon faces for B to copy. After 30 seconds or so, B takes the lead and A copies.
2. Children find a space. Ask them to walk through the space and to freeze in a demon shape when you give the word. Then they must move through the space silently as that demon. Repeat three times in a different demon shape and with different movements each time.
3. Sit the children down and ask for volunteers to show their demon shapes. Look at them, three or four at a time and solicit praise. Choose one or two volunteers and help them make the shape even more monstrous – does your demon have claws? Can you make your fingers look like claws? Can your demon be even more twisted? Has he got a pointed tongue? etc.
4. Children find a space again and work on their own individual shapes to make them as demonic as possible. Then ask them to sit in their space and to consider how they will move in the sea. How does the sea move? Solicit words such as *wave, rise and fall* and demonstrate how these movements might look. Can they show their monsters rising and falling like waves in the sea? Using a drum or a tambourine, have the children practise these movements at a gentle speed and at a stormy speed. As a control measure, you can emphasise that the movements should be on the spot, not across the floor.
5. Tell children they must remember these movements and sit them down in a circle. Produce the lengths of blue silk and ask them what they might represent (the sea). Demonstrate with a child how they can make the cloth move like a gentle wave. Have different children try this out in pairs, using all the cloths you have. Then demonstrate how this can be made to go faster in a controlled way. Again, let the children practise.

6. Sit the children in a circle and spread four cloths around the inside. Explain that everyone is to have a go at **performing** both as the sea and as the demons of the deep, moving both gently and stormily. Eight children will be using the cloths, while another seven or eight within the circle these cloths create will be the demons. They are to follow the lead from yourself using the drum or the bells as to whether they are to be stormy or becalmed. Three or four performances should allow for every child to be both sea and demon.

Assessment criteria
How controlled and expressive are the children's movements when representing the demons?
How controlled is their work with a partner when using the cloth to represent the sea?

Discussion/circle time

1. Do the children ever have nightmares? Would anyone like to share a scarey nightmare they have had with the class?
2. Should we be frightened of our nightmares?
3. What kind of things are the children frightened of? What kind of things is the teacher frightened of? Which of these things are actually harmless?
4. Do any of the children wish to share a story about a time when they were frightened?
5. What things *should* we be frightened of? Which of these can we avoid? Which can we deal with by telling someone about it?

Story: Sho and the Demons of the Deep
LESSON THREE

Key moral ideas
- Responsibility for the environment
- Laws and law breaking
- Group and individual responsibilities

Key learning objectives in drama
By the end of the lesson, children will have:
- questioned the teacher in role
- used language in role to argue, explain, question and persuade

Resources
Some silver coins; an empty scroll; flip chart and marker pen

Sequence of Activities

Note. Although the following activities are presented as one lesson, they are designed to be taught in 15-minute periods during class time over three successive days. They develop a consistent story and share the learning objectives described above. If you were to teach them as one drama lesson, you would need to consider ways of incorporating more physical activity and a greater variety of conventions.

1. Gather the children around you and tell them that they are about to have the chance to see and listen to one of the characters in the story of Sho. Tell them to watch and listen closely as you go into **teacher in role** as the refuse collector who took payment for ridding the village people of their demons only to dump them into the sea. Deliver a short monologue, counting your silver coins, pleased with your day's work and looking forward to doing the same again in other villages.

   Come out of role and ask the children whom they thought you were. Ask if there are any questions they would like to ask the refuse collector about his work or any comments they would like to make to him. List some of the questions and then let children **hot seat** you in role. Make your answers quite provocative. For example, if a child asks you if you really work for the Emperor, you might answer 'No, but people take me more seriously if I tell them that I do.' If they say that it's wrong to throw the demons into the sea, you might ask them why and then, when they have explained, say that you don't really care because you don't live near the sea yourself.

End the session by coming out of role and asking children what they think of the refuse collector and whether he ought to be allowed to carry on doing what he does or not. If not, why not?

2. Recap on yesterday's session and ask the children if they think they could pretend to be the people from Sho's village and persuade the Emperor to prevent the refuse collector from doing further damage. What kind of things might they tell him? Remind them that they must be very respectful to him and then go into **teacher in role** as the Emperor. Begin by asking them why they have come to see you and have them explain the problem thoroughly. Then act concerned but say that you're really not sure what you can do about it – do they have any ideas? Listen to all of their ideas and eventually say that, if he was breaking a law then you would be able to stop him. Could the children help you write a new law? With the children's help, write out this new law, incorporating their ideas, together with what they feel to be an appropriate punishment for breaking it. End the session by congratulating the children and obtain volunteers who will write it neatly on to a scroll for tomorrow's session.

3. Explain to the children that the Emperor has asked them to take this scroll around to the refuse collector. **In role** as the refuse collector, listen as it is read to you, then be surprised and perplexed. Why does the Emperor think what you have been doing is wrong? Can the villagers explain why it is so bad? Why shouldn't people be allowed to dump things where they want to? Make sure that the children as villagers thoroughly explain to you why what you do is wrong, then you might go sad and ask them how you can be expected to make a living. What other jobs are there to do with refuse collection that you might do? Listen to the children's suggestions and be very pleased when they come up with good ideas.

Assessment criteria
How well do the children hot seat the refuse collector in Activity 1? Are their questions relevant and do they listen and respond to the teacher's answers? How well do the children use language to persuade and help the Emperor in Activity 2; and to explain and argue with the refuse collector in Activity 3?

Discussion/circle time

1. Make a list of the good things the refuse collector did and the bad things that he did. Why are these things bad?
2. Why did the Emperor make a new law to stop the refuse collector? What do we mean by a 'law'?

3. In the story the refuse collector pollutes the sea by dumping the nightmare demons there. What do we mean by 'pollution'? In real life, how do seas and rivers get polluted? What effect does this have on the animals that live there?
4. Do the children ever see litter? Where? What kind of things do they see? Why is it bad to drop litter? When can it be harmful? What should we do with it?
5. What sort of things could the refuse collector usefully get rid of and where should he dump it all so that it will be harmless?

Literacy objectives and related activities

Pupils should be taught: **Fiction and Poetry**	*Examples from this chapter*
Reading comprehension 2. to investigate typical story themes, e.g. trials and forfeits, good over evil, weak over strong, wise over foolish;	*The class makes a database of the traditional tales they study this term and chart the features of each. Sho, for example, is weak but good and triumphant, whereas the demons are strong but evil and defeated.*
3. to identify and discuss main and recurring characters, evaluate their behaviour and justify views;	*The children discuss the behaviour of Sho, the demons and the refuse collector as integral parts of the drama and circle time activities.*
4. to choose and prepare poems for performance, identifying appropriate expression, tone, volume and use of voices and other sounds;	*Drama, Lesson 1*
5. rehearse and improve performance, taking note of punctuation and meaning;	*Children listen to the first recording of their reading in Lesson 1 and discuss how they can improve upon it for the second recording.*
Writing composition 7. to describe and sequence key incidents in a variety of ways, e.g. by listing, charting, mapping, making simple story boards;	*In groups of four or five, children are given one large sheet of paper and asked to make a **map of the story***

8. to write portraits of characters, using story text to describe behaviour and characteristics, and presenting portraits in a variety of ways, e.g. as posters, labelled diagrams, letters to friends about them;	*The work in Activity 7 is used as the basis for a large display. Children draw pictures of the main characters at different points of the story and attach them to the display at the appropriate geographical spaces. They select appropriate extracts from the story text to copy and attach next to these pictures.* *As one of the villagers, children write a letter describing how Sho rid them of the demons.*
10. to write alternative sequels to traditional stories using same characters and settings, identifying typical phrases and expressions from the story and using these to help structure the writing;	*Children write the story of how the villagers went to the Emperor and had him pass a law to stop the refuse collector.*
Non-fiction **Reading comprehension** 12. To identify the different purposes of instructional texts, e.g. . . . . rules;	*The teacher in role as Emperor guides children through the right kind of language needed to write a law. The children discuss the purpose of laws and write examples of the signposts that might be needed to discourage people from dumping refuse in the sea.*
14. how written instructions are organised, e.g. lists, numbered points . . .;	*The teacher in role as Emperor demonstrates how to incorporate these into the writing of the law if and when the children's ideas call for it.*
Word Level Work **Vocabulary extension** 24. to explore opposites, e.g. *upper/ lower, rude/polite*;	*Drama, Lesson 1, where children explore the opposites of words that describe monstrous behaviour.*

Year 4
Sweet Clara and the Freedom Quilt

Source:

Sweet Clara and the Freedom Quilt, Deborah Hopkinson, illustrated by James Ransome, 1995, Dragon Fly Books, New York.

National Literacy Strategy: Year 4 Term 3

Text Level Work

Fiction and Poetry
- Reading comprehension
  T1; T2
- Writing composition
  T8; T13; T14

Non-fiction
- Reading comprehension
  T16
- Writing composition
  T23

Social and Moral Themes

Friendship
- loneliness, being without friends

Rules
- laws and rules
- rights and responsibilities
- justice and fairness

Property and Power
- equality and inequality
- the value of property

Respecting Differences
- respecting racial and cultural differences
- respect and concern for others
- gender roles

Community
- working together
- group responsibilities

The story

Sweet Clara and the Freedom Quilt is the story of a 12-year-old black slave girl who is taken from her mother to work on a plantation south of the Ohio River. There she is cared for by Rachel, an older slave whom she calls her Aunt, and befriended by a young slave called Jack. Clara is frail and unlikely to survive as a field worker, so Aunt Rachel teaches her to sew and manages to have her employed as a seamstress in the owner's house. One day she overhears a conversation in the kitchen. The cook and two drivers are talking about the action the slave owners are taking to reduce the number of escape attempts. They mention how close by the Ohio River is, how the Underground Railroad will help those who make it across the river find freedom in Canada, how escape would be so much easier with a map. Later Clara questions Aunt Rachel about this conversation and is told about Canada and of how escapees follow the North Star to get there. She also explains to her what a map is. Clara then takes it upon herself to make a quilt that will act as a map. Saving up patches of scrap material and drawing upon information given her by Jack, whose own escape attempt has recently failed, she begins her quilt. As more of the slaves hear of her purpose and see the quality of her work, they begin to gather and contribute information about the surrounding geography. They tell her what crops are to be grown in which fields this year, how to find the track that will lead safely through a nearby swamp and other such details. When Clara finally completes her quilt she and Jack manage to escape, collecting Clara's mother and her new baby sister en route. The quilt, however, she leaves with Aunt Rachel who, though too old to escape herself, is thus able to help other slaves use it to escape to freedom.

Why this story?

- It provides an historically accurate picture of slavery in the southern United States but it avoids images of brutality inappropriate for young children.
- The slaves are not presented as victims to be pitied. Instead, they are seen as a supportive community in which they help one another survive and, when possible, find freedom. The story is therefore a story of hope.
- The story also provides strong images of girls, elderly women and of the non-nuclear family. These images are subtly woven into a strong narrative and are never intrusively 'politically correct'.
- The written text conveys the authentic rhythms, grammar and vocabulary of the black community and is supported by richly coloured illustrations that reinforce the values of the narrative.
- The story resembles the pattern of the classic hero quest story, referred to with reference to Year 1 work. However, here the hero is the frailest person in the story. She triumphs not through strength, impetuousness and violence but through cunning, patience and artistry. She also acts as an agent to activate communal action rather than as a celebration of individual action. The values of the story are, as with the story of Sho, a healthy contrast to many of the tales of heroism children will come across, particularly on film and video. The quilt itself is a powerful image of these values – a female, communal, creative form of resistance.

The drama

The drama begins on Home Plantation after Clara and Jack have escaped. For the children, it is meant to unfold as an adventure, a story of escape, danger, risks to be overcome and ultimate triumph as the slaves eventually reach the Ohio River and freedom. The work is structured, however, to reinforce the community values so clearly at the heart of the book; the need to work together, to help one another, to support one another through difficulty. The rules the children, in role as runaways, agree to stick to, are meant to underline these values, and the dilemmas and difficulties they meet on their journey are set against this background of shared purpose and communal action. The quilt they create together in the initial lesson is, as in the book itself, a visual symbol of this. The sessions as presented are best taught in a large space such as the hall, but can be adapted for the classroom. Each session as written is between 1 hour 15 minutes and 1 hour 30 minutes in length.

Why this drama?

- The story and literacy work in Week 1 will provide a strong historical and geographical context, the details of which can inform and be reinforced by the subsequent drama work.
- The journey to freedom is significant in the book but there is little narrative action or adventure on the way. This kind of narrative gap provides a good space for drama.
- Journeys are a well-tried and tested structural framework for exciting and provocative drama with children. In particular, the adventures can present a testing ground for the children by presenting them with different moral dilemmas. They can also meet different characters on the way, who can present good or bad examples of ethical action for them to reflect upon.
- There are powerful symbols in the story that lend themselves readily to drama. The North Star represents hope, the quilt the values of communality and creativity mentioned above, the journey to the Ohio River the quest for freedom. Not only do such symbols help give shape to drama work, their representation can help children understand their significance and begin to master the workings of symbol.

Proposed timescale for work: 4 weeks

Week 1	Week 2	Week 3	Week 4
The book *Literacy hour* *Circle time*	Preparing for the drama: Drama: Session 1 Extended writing *Literacy hour* *Additional English time* *Circle time*	Drama: Session 2 Extended writing *Literacy hour* *Additional English time* *Circle time*	Drama: Session 3 Extended writing *Literacy hour* *Additional English time* *Circle time*

Week 1

Literacy objectives and related activities

Pupils should be taught: **Fiction and Poetry**	***Examples for work deriving from the book.***
Reading comprehension 1. to identify social, moral or cultural issues in stories, e.g. dilemmas faced in the story or the moral of the story, and to discuss how the characters deal with them; to locate evidence in text;	*List examples from the text of the injustices suffered by slaves.* *Why does Clara need help in the early parts of the story? Which people look after her and how?* *List the different ways that the slaves support and help one another in the story.*
2. to read stories from other cultures, by focusing on e.g differences in place, time, customs, relationships; to identify and discuss recurring themes where appropriate;	*In how many ways is Clara's life on Home Plantation different from the way the children live?*
Writing composition 8. to write critically about an issue or dilemmas raised in a story, explaining the problem, alternative courses of action and the writer's solution;	*Explain why slaves such as Jack wanted to run away but explain the dangers they faced when they did. Why was Clara's map so helpful?*
Non-fiction **Reading comprehension** 16. to read, compare and evaluate examples of arguments and discussions, e.g. letters to press, articles, discussion of issues in books, e.g. environment, animal welfare;	*The teacher writes a letter to the paper in the voice of a member of the Underground Railroad, explaining why they think slavery is wrong. Children read and discuss this.*

Writing composition	
23. to present a point of view in writing, e.g. in the form of a letter, a report or a script, linking points persuasively and selecting style and vocabulary appropriate to the reader;	*Use one of these forms to present an account of the evils of slavery to a particular audience – the owner of Home Plantation, for example.*

Discussion/circle time

1. Clara is physically weak but she helps many slaves escape. What skill does she develop to do this? What skills do the children have? What skills could they develop? Could any of these skills help others? How?

2. Aunt Rachel is too old to escape herself. But does this mean that she is of no use to others? Encourage children to talk of times when an old person has helped them in some way. Why should we value old people?

3. Compare how the owners of Home Plantation lived to the way the slaves lived. Why was it unfair? Did it mean they were better people than the slaves? Why not?

4. At the start of the story, Clara is a newcomer to the plantation, unhappy, and alone. How is she made to feel better? Can children recall any time when they have felt lonely and when someone was friendly to them? Or when they were friendly to someone they could see felt unhappy? How did this make them feel?

Week 2

Preparing for the drama: Making the quilt

You need to have the following prepared in advance:
- A large rectangular sheet of paper divided into squares of 15 cm^2 each. There should be the same number of squares as there are children in your class. Each square should be marked with an individual child's name. Mark in Home Plantation in the bottom left hand corner and the Ohio River in the top right hand corner (see Figure 1.3). Mount the paper on the wall.
- Sheets of paper, 15 cm^2 each, one for each child.
- Small pieces of paper with a geographical feature specified in each. These should be folded and placed in two separate hats. As the squares on the quilt alternate between cultivated and uncultivated land, one hat should contain different crops for different fields, the other different landmarks. (See Activity 3 below and illustration of class quilt (Figure 1.4).)

1. Look at the double page illustration in the book of the quilt Clara made. Ask the children if they can spot any of the things mentioned in the story. In particular, they should be able to spot the Ohio River; the boat hidden on the bank; the North Star; a village; the swamp; the broken tree.

2. Turn to the pre-prepared outline for the quilt/map on the wall. Explain to the children that they are to create their own map. Beginning with a child whose square is adjacent to Home Plantation, have them mark a track in their square only. The child whose square the track leads into must continue it. Encourage children to mark in other tracks and streams, too, as can be seen on Clara's quilt. The main track needs to conclude at the Ohio River.

3. Once these details are completed, the large sheet can act as a template for the final quilt. Children can now be given their individual squares of paper. The alternating arrangement of the quilt should make it evident which children need to design a cultivated and which an uncultivated square. For the uncultivated squares, there need to be a variety of features. If there are 30 children in your class, for example, you will need 15 squares of paper with a feature named on each. These might include: *3 villages; 3 farmhouses; 2 swamps; 3 woods; a graveyard; a church; a hill; an old barn.* The existence of populated areas, of potential hazards and hiding places, is important for the drama that follows.

4. Children find out the feature that needs to be drawn in their own square by drawing a paper from the hat. You might refer children to the illustration of Clara's quilt for ideas as to how these might be drawn.

5. For those children who are to illustrate the cultivated fields, the slips of paper can indicate a variety of different coloured plants that might grow in the fields along with the cotton or corn, such as daisies, cornflowers, poppies and grass. The squared pattern for illustrating these fields can be adapted from the book (see Figure 1.4).

6. Once children are aware of what should go into their square, they can draw and colour it. Make sure that those children with tracks and streams copy exactly what they marked on the template. Once the squares are finished, glue them onto the large sheet to complete the quilted map you will use in the subsequent drama

Preparing for the drama: News from Clara and Jack

As part of your literacy or English work, explain to the children that, although most slaves were not allowed to be taught to read or write, some managed to learn and could sometimes obtain copies of newspapers circulated secretly by the Underground Railroad. As these were circulated among so many people, however, they were often damaged and torn. Show them a copy of Figure 1.5, enlarged for the OHP. Explain how it reached Aunt Rachel in this condition. Can they help complete the missing sentences with their important advice for any slaves considering escape? It is important to have this completed list ready for the first drama lesson.

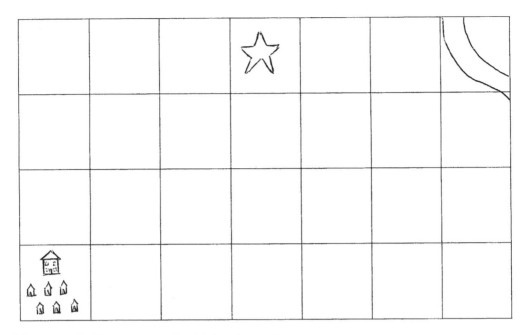

Figure 1.3 Pre-prepared grid for the quilt map

Figure 1.4 The quilt map

ANOTHER TWO SLAVES ARE FREE!

The Underground Railroad helps them escape.

Two young slaves crossed the Ohio River last night into freedom.
Their names are Clara and Jack and they had these words of advice for anyone thinking of following them.

'Avoid going near towns and farms because you don't want to be

'Don't try to steal anything on the journey because

'Travel only by night because

'Above all, stick together bec

'Share what you have with

'Look after one an

Figure 1.5 Newspaper report of escape by Clara and Jack

Story: Sweet Clara and the Freedom Quilt
DRAMA: ONE

Key moral ideas
- Working together
- Group responsibilities

Learning objectives in drama
By the end of the lesson, children will have:
- sustained work in role for most of the lesson
- helped sustain tension and atmosphere through carefully controlled use of movement and voice

Resources
Copy of Figure 1.5 written large, with Clara's rules of advice in their completed form.
One or two torches.
Simple items of costume, such as a shawl, for Aunt Rachel and a hat or stick for the overseer.
Mats to mark out the cabins.

Sequence of Activities	*Commentary*
1. Initial warm-up **game**. Have mats spread around the perimeter of the hall. The children are to move in space and at the call 'To your cabins' they must gather in groups of five on the mats for a 'group hug'. The aim is to avoid being the last group to do it. After two or three rounds, specify that each group must contain at least two girls or two boys. At the end of the final game, inform children that the groups now on each mat will form their cabin groups for the drama. Give each group a number.	*The aim here is to get children into mixed ability and gender groups they have not chosen themselves and with whom they must work regularly throughout the drama. You may need to alter the rules according to the number of boys/girls in the class.*

2. Sit the children around the teacher's chair and introduce the items of costume, inviting them to speculate on the characters they might represent. Look carefully at selected illustrations from the book and discuss what jobs the slaves had to do on Home Plantation. Share the jobs out among the children and divide the space into zones, e.g. where the housework went on; where the work in the fields went on. You might also indicate the space that represents Aunt Rachel's cabin.

Children should also be reminded of the work done in the literacy hour that explored the differences between life on Home Plantation and life today. They need to remember, in particular, that there was little machinery and that slaves did all the menial jobs by hand.

3. Children move to the appropriate zones and **mime** their jobs in the space. **Narrate** how hot it could be, how the overseer would often patrol and check that the jobs were being done properly and that the slaves were working hard enough. **In role** as the overseer, move about and question them about their work, urging them to work harder.

Be brisk and business-like as the overseer, rather than aggressive. You might mention that there is to be a party at the big house tomorrow and that the mistress wants everything at its best.

4. **Narrate** how the slaves were always very tired at the end of the day when they returned to their cabins, how they would often lie and look out of the window at the North Star and think of Clara and Jack. Dim the lights and shine the torch on to a wall to represent the North Star. **Thought track** some individuals as to what they are thinking in role.

Some children may need questions to prompt them here.

5. **In role** as Aunt Rachel, give a secret signal to each cabin in turn – three hoots of an owl, or flashes from the lamp for cabin three; four for cabin four, etc. At their signal, children move as quietly as possible to her cabin. They sit so that they can all see the 'quilt' spread out before them. Address the **meeting** in hushed tones and inform them that tonight is the night the slaves must escape. The journey to the Ohio River will take two nights – they will need to camp/hide during the daylight hours. Help the children decide where the best place for this camp will be. Point to a village or dwelling near this place and tell them there is a doctor there whom, you have heard, could be a friend to runaway slaves. Each of them must take one item of food or drink to share with everyone in their cabin. Above all, they are to remember Clara's advice. As Aunt Rachel, you can't read – can anyone here read? Have volunteers read through the rules before they leave in their groups and have different cabins memorise a rule each. The groups return silently to their cabins as their number is whispered.

6. Back in their cabins, children can be asked to include a small personal item to take with them, without telling anyone what it is. Each group then **acts out** their escape.

The game to get children to Aunt Rachel's cabin should heighten tension and calls for attention, concentration and control.

Refer to the quilt/map to show exactly where they will all be heading. Mark out the track they should take, calling on the children who designed the different squares to share their knowledge of dangers, landmarks, etc.

This is important as the doctor will feature in the next session.

Some classes may need discussion out of role about the kind of food that the slaves would be able to take – no cans, for example!
As with the sharing of the food, the sharing of the responsibility to learn the rules emphasises the advantages of working as a team.

The escape can be orchestrated by Aunt Rachel's signal.

7. Finish with a **sculpted image** of Aunt Rachel, gazing after the run-aways. **Thought track** the possible questions that might be running through her mind at this instant.	*A child can volunteer to be sculpted into a number of possibilities before choosing one.* *Have two torches and ask two children to create the North Star by shining their beams together on the wall.*

Assessment criteria
How well do children work in their allocated groups?
Can they sustain the role play and the atmosphere throughout the duration of the drama work?

Literacy objectives and related activities

Pupils should be taught: **Fiction and Poetry**	*Examples emanating from the drama*
Writing composition 13. to write own longer stories in chapters from story plans;	*Write Chapter 1 of the story of the escape, to be told in three chapters, in the first person. The plan for this chapter could include: a brief autobiography; life at Home Plantation; the meeting with Aunt Rachel; an account of the escape.*
14. to write poems, experimenting with different styles and structures, discuss if and why different forms are more suitable than others;	*Use the thoughts of Aunt Rachel as she gazes at the North Star as the basis for a poem entitled 'Star of Hope'. The possibilities for writing it as a shape poem can be discussed and explored.*

Discussion/circle time

1. What examples in their own lives can children think of that illustrate the importance of agreeing on rules; of sticking together; of trusting one another? (*sports/games are a good example; examples from school or other aspects of community life*)
2. Why do the children think that slave owners did not want slaves to learn how to read and write? What things does *not* being able to read and write prevent you from doing?
3. What did the children choose as special possessions to take with them in the drama? In what sense are such possessions valuable to the owner?

Story: Sweet Clara and the Freedom Quilt
DRAMA: TWO

Key moral ideas
- Rights and responsibilities
- Equality and inequality
- Justice and fairness

Learning objectives in drama
By the end of the lesson, children will have:
- confronted and grappled with the complexities of a moral dilemma through sustained role play
- presented a possible resolution in the form of a short play

Resources
Costume; hat/bag (for doctor)

Sequence of Activities	Commentary
1. Begin the lesson with a warm-up game, if appropriate. Recap on the drama so far and recall where the runaways were to make their first camp.	*Children may well need help in remembering the rules each cabin had to learn. The fact that the slaves had no money needs emphasising at this point, too.*
2. Refer to the quilt and talk of the possible dangers the slaves might have faced on their first night's journey. In their groups, ask the children to create and show a **still image** to illustrate one danger they faced and how they all worked together to overcome it.	*These dangers may lurk in the swamp or in the populated villages. It is also important for the subsequent drama that children are aware of the location of the nearest habitation to their camp.*
3. Select one of the groups and ask the class to suggest ways in which their image might be changed to show what would have happened if the danger had *not* been averted. How would the group have helped their friend make it to the encampment? Ask children to imagine that this group was unfortunate and that this is indeed what happened. Where could the slaves get help?	*It is important for the succeeding drama to choose a group here whose danger will result in injury rather than death.* *Children should remember Aunt Rachel telling them of the doctor that might be a friend who lives nearby.*

4. Sit the children in a circle and set up the scene where the doctor's help is sought. Have the children decide how many will go to his surgery. Play the scene in the circle with **teacher in role** as the doctor. The children call at your surgery. Agree to examine the patient and tell the slaves to bring him to the surgery. You are aware that they are escaped slaves. Say that they can all hide in your barn where they will be safe during the daylight hours.

Play the role of the doctor ambiguously and build the tension here – let the children know that you are aware they are runaway slaves and hesitate before agreeing to help. Emphasise that it will soon be light and they will be seen if they don't hurry. Perhaps you are expecting the sheriff to call, which makes it imperative that they wait for your signal before bringing in their injured comrade.

5. **Narrate** 'The slaves all returned to the barn and waited. But later, when the doctor came to see them, he was on his own.' **In role**, tell them that you have treated their friend who is safe now but in need of rest; and that, in two or three days time, you will be taking him back to Home Plantation. This will be the only way you can obtain a fee for your work. The slave's health in exchange for his freedom seems like a fair exchange. Argue this with the children but remain implacable.

The shock of the doctor's decision should provoke a lot of argument from the children. Some may offer you their precious possessions – but they are of no possible value to you. Some may offer to take the injured party's place, in which case you may question as to how strong and hardworking they are. The injured slave would, of course, slow the rest of the party down. And, although you have saved them from the sheriff once, you won't do so again, etc.

6. Stop the drama and discuss with the children the choices now open to the runaways. Some of these can be explored through **forum theatre** or various options can be acted out and illustrated in **short plays** by the different groups.

Stop the drama before a resolution is reached and allow children to explore and decide upon possible outcomes themselves. Refer them to their rules for guidance. If they present their ideas as a short play, provide clear structural guidelines, e.g. no longer than 30 seconds in length.

7. Finish on a cliff-hanger – which of these possibilities actually happened? We shall find out next time and we shall also find out if the slaves *did* manage to escape.	*There may well be a general consensus that emerges across the group work, in which case you can draw upon specific details that different groups present to inform the work in the next session.*

Assessment criteria

How seriously do the children approach the dilemma through their role play?

What arguments do they use against the doctor in role?

What actions do they deem appropriate for the runaways?

Literacy hour/English time

Write the second chapter of their escape story. Rather than simply narrating the events, you might ask some children to relate one section of this week's drama in detail, trying hard to capture the atmosphere of tension.

Discussion/circle time

1. Discuss the nature of the dilemma the slaves faced in the drama and the action they chose to take. Were they right to do this? Were there alternatives?
2. Can children talk of a time when they were injured and someone helped them?
3. What do the children think of the doctor's actions? List the good things and the bad things that he did/said. Why do they think he behaved as he did? List what they think makes a good doctor.
4. What services do the children think everyone ought to be entitled to, free of charge? Why? Where does the money come from to pay their doctors and teachers?

Story: Sweet Clara and the Freedom Quilt
DRAMA: THREE

Key moral ideas
- Trust and loyalty
- Working together

Learning objectives in drama
By the end of the lesson, children will have:
- created still images to convey emotion and tension as well as narrative meaning
- used role once again to explore a moral dilemma
- used a mix of planned play making and improvisation to attempt to resolve the dramatic problem

Resources
Quilt; old scarf for slave; hat and 'gun' (a stick) for the patroller

Sequence of Activities	Commentary
1. Choose a warm-up game, if appropriate, then recap on the previous session. Reflect together upon which of the rules were kept or broken.	
2. Look at the quilt and the journey facing the slaves on their second and final night of flight. Talk about any new dangers they may now face as a result of their encounter with the doctor.	*Talk in particular about areas where a patroller might be looking for them. Will the sheriff be more likely to know of their whereabouts now?*
3. In their cabin groups, the children show a **still image** to illustrate how they were nearly caught by a patroller. The image should aim to indicate place (where on the quilt did this happen?) and tension (in body and facial expression). One child in each group represents the patroller.	*These images are shown and interrogated – how can we tell where this is? What do you think X is thinking? How can we tell from her body/face? etc.*

4. Choose one of these images, ask the children to remain still but take on the role of the patroller yourself. Alter the image so that the patroller sees one of the slaves and speak something like the following **in role**: 'I've got you covered, now just move out of there very slowly, out into the middle of this clearing. You're not going anywhere until it's light. Then we'll be heading back to Home Plantation. Don't try anything stupid. I'm already jumpy enough.'

You can make these lines fit the geography of the particular image – perhaps the slaves are in a wood, or a graveyard, etc. You might also slip in some lines that the children might feel able to exploit later; perhaps you are frightened of the dark, of evil spirits, etc.

5. Call the children together and sit this group to the side, near you. 'Let's suppose that, when all the runaways assembled near the boat later that night, one group never arrived. However, one of their number had slipped away unnoticed and made his way to the Ohio River.' Choose a volunteer from the group and begin a **meeting**, yourself **in role** as a slave, first of all asking the child to narrate what had happened. The slaves have a choice: either they escape now or they attempt to rescue their comrades.

Whatever ideas the children come up with to rescue their friends, be adamant that it is pointless to attempt the rescue in a way that will lead inevitably to loss of life. Emphasise the need for cunning and end the meeting only when you think the difficulties, possibilities and choices have been well-aired.

6. Set up an image of the captured group in the clearing. They are so close to the Ohio River and yet so far from freedom. They can hear the sounds of the rushing water and it seems to be whispering phrases to them – what are they? **Sculpt the image**, with the captives looking at the North Star. The rest of the class then creates the **sound collage** softly. You can then **thought track** the children representing the slaves in the image.

*You might also create a **parallel image** of Aunt Rachel, awoken from a bad dream, she, too, looking at the North Star.*

7. Children now work out a course of action in their cabin groups. Hear their plans one at a time and then explain that they will be tested one at a time. Ask each group to rehearse the initial stages of their plan.

If any groups decide to go ahead and attempt to escape on their own, you can still, in the next activity, take on the role of patroller on the banks of the river and make things difficult for them!

8. Set up a performance space and sit the children around it. Each attempted rescue is improvised in turn with **teacher in role** as the patroller. Some groups may succeed, some may fail.

*This is a type of **forum theatre**. You need to improvise what you do as patroller from what the children give you. Encourage children to learn from the success or failure of each group by discussing between each attempt.*

9. As a final exercise, the escaped slaves reassemble in their groups on the opposite bank of the Ohio River. Now it is time for them to go their separate ways. What words of farewell do they offer one another? **Narrate** how, for years afterwards, whether alone or with friends, they could never see the North Star without remembering their escape, the friends that survived, those that didn't, Aunt Rachel back at Home Plantation, holding the quilt and gazing up at the North Star and smiling. Create this image to conclude the drama.

These can be heard in turn or you can ask children to speak them at will.

Assessment criteria

How well do the children convey emotion and tension in the images created in Activities 3 and 6?

How effectively do the children explore the dilemma in Activity 5?

How well do the children improvise with the teacher in role in Activity 8?

Literacy hour/English time

Children write the concluding chapter to their escape story.

Discussion/circle time

1. Can children think of examples from their own lives when a friend has stuck by them when it would have been easier not to? Or when they stuck by a friend?
2. Ask the children to help you list examples of the good and bad things different people did during the drama of the slaves' escape. Discuss why the children think they were good/bad.

Year 5
The Sea Woman

Source:

British Folk Tales, Kevin Crossley-Holland, 1987, Orchard Books, London.

National Literacy Strategy: Year 5 Term 2	**Social and Moral Themes**
Text Level Work Fiction and Poetry ● Reading comprehension 　**T1; T2; T3; T5; T8** ● Writing composition 　**T11; T13** Non-fiction ● Reading comprehension 　**T14**	*Friendship* ● bullying *Rules* ● blame, guilt and feeling sorry ● intention and responsibility ● justice and fairness *Property and Power* ● equality and inequality ● ownership of property *Respecting Differences* ● respecting racial and cultural differences ● respect and concern for others ● empathy for those in different circumstances ● gender roles *Community and Environment* ● belonging and not belonging

The story

There are numerous versions of the story of *The Sea Woman*, sometimes referred to as *The Seal Woman* or *The Selkie Bride*. They originate from northern, Celtic islands and tell of the selkies, a people who live as seals in the sea but who can, by removing their skins, take human form on land. They therefore inhabit a marginal territory, belonging to both land and sea. But if the fishing communities from which the story originates belonged more to the land, then the selkies were their mirror image, belonging more to the sea.

   In the version of the story I use, as retold by Kevin Crossley-Holland, a lonely fisherman surprises a group of sea people dancing in the moonlight and captures the skin of one of them, a young and beautiful woman. Refusing her pleas for him to hand the skin back to her, which would enable her to return to her family in the sea, he leads her back to his cottage and hides the skin in a haystack in a nearby field. The Sea Woman thus has no choice but to stay with the fisherman, eventually marrying him and giving birth to three children, a girl and two boys. They look just the same as other children apart from the fact that they each have their mother's eyes – wide, sea eyes, flint grey in colour; and they each have small transparent webs between their fingers and toes. She loves her children but can often be seen to return to a rock on the shore from where she sings a sad song that she shares with a large seal who surfaces close to her. Then, one afternoon her children are playing in the field and accidentally discover the skin in a haystack. Not knowing what it is, they take it to their mother who hesitates briefly, hugs each of them in turn and then runs from the house. When she reaches the shore she pulls on the skin and dives into the sea, where she is joined by a large seal and they circle and leap together before disappearing under the water. When the fisherman returns and later finds his children, still gazing out over the sea, he tells them to wait for him at home and wades out into the sea, where the Sea Woman surfaces to speak to him for the last time. She tells him that she must return to her first, true husband and asks him to care for their children as she has done, before diving and disappearing forever.

Why this story?

- Crossley-Holland's version is beautifully told, highly evocative of the rugged, cold, harsh life of the isolated fishing community. The language is rich in its poetic qualities and economical in its narrative.
- The story's qualities of magic and mystery appeal to children of this age and they are often moved by its haunting melancholy and the ambiguity of its resolution.
- In the tale, a woman has her freedom violated by a man. She lives in a culture where she can never feel at home and, when given the choice, she opts to leave her children to be true to herself. The story therefore resonates symbolically with issues of difference, of identity, of choice and power in gender relationships, issues pertinent to contemporary living that impinge on social and family life and therefore on many children's lives. The fact that these issues remain in the realm of myth adds an additional, protective quality to their fictional treatment.
- There are other versions of the tale, both from western and other cultural sources, that this version can be compared to.

The drama

The drama work is presented in three clear sections. The first two explore issues emerging from the story itself. The third section, comprising two lessons, creates a new story, a possible sequel to the original. The second and third sections are best done in a hall but they have been adapted and successfully taught in classrooms.

1. *Introductory activities*: these include and follow closely the first telling of the tale and could be done quite easily in most classrooms. They can be easily worked into the literacy hour.
2. *An exploration of the symbolisms of the tale (Drama session 1). (Approximately 1 hour)* This leads to a shared performance that could be developed to form part of a class assembly.

3. *A sequel to the tale (Drama sessions 2 and 3).* This is presented in the form of two lesson plans, each of about 1 hour/1 hour 15 minutes in length.

Why this drama work?

- The work in the first two sessions will help children approach the sometimes painful emotional content of the story through the protection of art and symbol. It is only through such an approach that the moral dimensions of the tale can be tapped into.
- The work in the second session, in particular, allows children to explore the possibilities of symbol and symbolisation.
- There is a strong sense of a possible future to the story, a 'what if . . .?' scenario, always a good space for drama work. One of the issues the story explores is that of cultural difference; but the children of the Sea Woman are also, in a symbolic sense, ethnically different. So what if, after the Sea Woman had left, there were moves from the king to ethnically cleanse the island? What effect might this have on the sea children and how would the other children on the island react? The drama can explore these issues, sadly relevant to our contemporary world, without articulating them in specific racial or ethnic terms.

Proposed time scale for work: 3–4 weeks

Week 1	Week 2	Week 3	Week 4
The story Introductory drama activities Drama Session 1 Discussion *Literacy hour Additional English time Circle time*	Drama: Session 2 Extended writing Discussion *Literacy hour Additional English time Circle time*	Drama: Session 3 Extended writing Discussion *Literacy hour Additional English time Circle time*	Conclude writing (if necessary) *Additional English time*

Week 1

The initial week's work is presented in the following order:
1. Introductory drama activities.
2. Drama: Session 1.
3. Table of NLS objectives with related activities.
4. Topics for discussion/circle time.

Introductory drama activities

These can be taught as one lesson or can be spread over two or three sessions of the literacy hour.

Activity	Commentary
Key moral ideas: • Empathy with those in different circumstances • Power, fairness and gender roles.	
Gather the children together and tell them the tale orally.	*It is important to tell the tale and not read it. Do not learn it by heart but use some key phrases and images and keep the tone of your tale similar to the original.*
With the class, list ten key points from the story to act as a prompt for anyone trying to retell the tale. Display these clearly, then choose five children, or ask for five volunteers, who will act as the storytellers. Divide the rest of the class into equal groups and attach each group to a storyteller. As the storyteller tells the tale the other children **act it out** spontaneously. The storytellers are allowed to improvise additional details if they want, so long as they stay true to the plot.	*There are a variety of ways of using narrative storytelling and improvisation. This is rather a sophisticated method and is only likely to work if children have had previous experience of similar, more teacher-directed approaches. See notes in Appendix 2 on using the* **story wand** *for help.*
Ask the children to consider what might be the worst possible moment in the story for the Sea Woman. In groups of five, ask them to create a **still image** of this, showing clearly how and why it is a terrible moment for her. Interrogate each image, concentrating children's attention on interpreting how it signals that the moment is so bad.	*There are four or five possibilities that children can normally think of and you might like to discuss these with the whole class in advance and share them out.*

Story: The Sea Woman
DRAMA: LESSON ONE

Key moral ideas
- Belonging and not belonging
- Intention and responsibility
- Blame, guilt and feeling sorry

Learning objectives in drama
By the end of the lesson, children will have:
- made visual, symbolic meanings relevant to the tale, using netting material
- created and carried out a simple whole class performance

Resources
Five two-metre lengths of thin black netting; one two-metre length of white netting.
Slow, atmospheric music, for example by Enya, Clannad or Alan Stivell.

Sequence of Activities	Commentary
1. Begin with a movement game. Children move freely in the space and freeze on the signal into sharp, jagged shapes, like the rocks on the coast of the island. At each freeze, children can be asked to vary their level and shape.	*Children will benefit from being shown pictures of the Scottish coastline beforehand and describing/ discussing its rugged nature.*
2. Sit the children in a circle and place a piece of the black netting in the centre. Ask the children what it might represent from the story. Children are likely to suggest the skin and one of the fisherman's nets. Encourage them then to make a symbolic link between the two. Invite children to come out and explore how we can represent this symbolic meaning, i.e. how we can show the skin transforming into a net used by the fisherman to trap the Sea Woman.	*You can do this by asking them to think about how the fisherman normally catches things from the sea (by holding a net) and how he catches the Sea Woman (by holding her skin).*

3. Put children into groups of five and ask them to play with and then to create one of these symbolic images with the netting.	*The time for play is important, particularly if children are unused to working with cloth/material.*
4. View what the children produce and encourage positive comments from the class. Then show them the piece of white netting and ask what this reminds them of (a wedding veil). Ask how the wedding veil is another way the fisherman entraps the Sea Woman. Encourage them to notice the difference between a black veil (for mourning) and a white veil (for a wedding) and ask them why the black veil might suit the Sea Woman's feelings on her wedding day. Ask the groups to use the net to create a brief moving image of her wedding and to work out ways of moving from this image into the image they created in Activity 3.	*The wedding veil and these references to colour are culturally specific so you will need, of course, to take account of the ethnic and cultural mix of your class when asking these questions. However, the story is a western story so it is valid to encourage children to work with these symbols.* *Encourage and praise clarity of image through use of gesture and facial expression. Encourage movement to be structured, rehearsed and as economical as possible.*
5. Introduce children to the music. Ask them to consider why you have chosen it to accompany their work. Ask them to adapt their movement to fit with the music in terms of pace and emotional content. They need, too, to find a way to move into the first image. When these have been rehearsed, **perform** them altogether, then one at a time to the music.	*It is important that the music you choose fits the setting and the mood of the story – slow, melancholy, Celtic.* *You might allow children to view one another's work half a class at a time, asking them to pick out moments that they particularly liked.*

6. On the board or a flip chart, have two columns headed 'you should have' and 'you shouldn't have'. Under each heading have children list what the fisherman might be thinking as he stands in the waves at the end of the story. 'You should have let her go free', for example, or 'You should never have taken her skin'.

You might begin this by briefly discussing the ending of the story. In what ways are the various people unhappy? Whom do the children think is ultimately responsible?

7. Ask children to consider this image of the fisherman and ask for a volunteer to be **sculpted** into a position that represents him standing in the waves. Have the rest of the class sit around him and softly make a **sound collage** of the sounds of the wind and the sea. Speculate that the fisherman imagines he can hear voices in the waves. Ask half the class to choose a line from the 'should have' list, the other half from the 'shouldn't have' list. Have the children repeat this image, intermittently interrupting the sound collage by whispering these phrases softly but distinctly at will.

Unless the children are used to such work, they will need help in exploring possible ways of making these sounds. It may help if you 'conduct' the sound, particularly its volume.

8. You may add this image to the beginning of the work performed in Activity 5 and repeat the performance to conclude the lesson.

Assessment criteria

Do the children understand the potential of the netting to create symbolic images?

How clear and expressive are the images they create? Do they convey an emotional impact?

Do their suggestions in Activity 6 show an appreciation of the moral impact of the fisherman's decisions throughout the tale?

Literacy objectives and related activities

Pupils should be taught: **Fiction and Poetry**	***Examples from 'Sea Woman' work, Week 1***
Reading comprehension 1. to identify and classify the features of myths, legends and fables, e.g. the moral in a fable, fantastical beasts in legends;	*Include this tale among those from which you build up the classificatory list over the term, e.g. categorise* selkie *among animals that can take human form; creatures that are half-animal, half-human, etc.*
2. to investigate different versions of the same story, identifying similarities and differences; recognise how stories change over time and differences of culture and place that are expressed in stories;	*Compare this version to:* ● *other versions, e.g. Shirley Hughes' 'The Selkie Bride' in 'Stories by Firelight';* ● *versions from other cultures, e.g. 'The Swan Maiden', in 'The Classic Fairy Tales' edited by Maria Tatar.* *Begin a reading of Berlie Docherty's 'Daughter of the Sea' and discuss the similarities of setting and theme.*
3. to explore similarities and differences between oral and written storytelling;	*Children discuss the differences between the written version and the oral version you told the class. Which phrases/details did you include? Which did you change or leave out? Were there any strategies you used to help remember the tale and keep it flowing that are absent from the written version?*
5. to perform poems in a variety of ways;	*Children write poems based on the work in Drama: Lesson One above. Experiment with incorporating the visual and aural imagery of this session into group presentations of these poems. Discuss their effectiveness as performance.*

8. to distinguish between the author and the narrator, investigating narrative viewpoint and the treatment of different characters, e.g. minor characters, heroes, villains and perspectives on the action from different characters;	*The still image work in the introductory drama.* *The perspective of the fisherman, as explored in the final image of Drama: Lesson One.*
14. make notes of story outline as preparation for oral storytelling;	*As in the second introductory drama activity.*

Discussion/circle time

1. When do we feel sorry for the Sea Woman during the story? Why?
2. In what ways does the Sea Woman come to belong to the fisherman? In what ways does she never belong to him? Where does she belong?
3. Do you feel you belong somewhere or with some particular group of people? Where and when do you feel this most strongly?
4. Who is unhappy at the end of the story? Do we think the fisherman thought the story would end this way when he captured the Sea Woman? Who do we think is most to blame for this unhappiness, the Sea Woman or the fisherman? Why?
5. What do we mean by 'selfishness'? Can our selfishness make others unhappy, even though we don't mean to?

Week 2

Story: The Sea Woman
DRAMA: LESSON TWO

Key moral ideas
- Prejudice and discrimination
- Concern for others

Learning objectives in drama
By the end of the lesson, children will have:
- sustained a role and contributed to the maintenance of dramatic tension
- speculated and contributed to the development of the story's plot
- used and experienced language to persuade

Resources
Walking stick; small leather pouch with coins

Sequence of Activities	Commentary
1. **Warm-up.** Ask children to creep as silently as possible through the space, having them freeze when you give the signal. Explain that this will be part of a story we will make together today.	
2. Sit the children in a semi-circle and recap the end of the story of *The Sea Woman*. Explain that together you will be making a play that will explore events that took place on the island a year later.	*Contract the rules of the drama, control strategies, teacher-in-role, etc.*
3. Tell the class that you are going to imagine that there was a small school on this island which all the children attended. It was at the other end of the island, about 30 minutes on foot from the fisherman's cottage, which was solitary and isolated. Explain that you are going see a **preview** of	*The preview is a way of engaging children's interest. It is necessarily ambiguous so your own role and the role of the children in the image remain unexplained at this point. However, the children should quickly recognise that someone is looking for the sea children and can speculate who and why before the*

the new story. The setting is the school hall. Have four volunteers stand at the front, holding out their hands and staring ahead. **In role**, examine their hands and eyes, then dismiss them, silently. Come out of role and ask the class to try to interpret this image.

drama proper begins in the next activity.

4. Begin **in role** as the adviser to the King of the mainland, the children in role as the children who live on the island. Inform them who you are and that you are on a mission from the King. He has discovered some disturbing news – that some of his subjects are the children of unnatural mothers who come from the sea. The strange colour of their eyes and the webs on the fingers give them away. You have examined everyone here, but can the children tell you if and where you can find some of these 'sea children'? The King will reward anyone who will help him. Show them the bag of coins and question one or two children individually. Eventually admit that you know that there are three such children on the island and that you have soldiers camped out on the beach who will search every house and cottage for them tomorrow, beginning at dawn.

Play the adviser as someone who does not have to raise his voice to exercise his power and as someone the children will not trust. If questioned about what the King has in mind for the sea children, be evasive – they will be removed to somewhere safe but out of the way, etc. Build up the tension by letting out what you know only a little at a time in your questioning of individual children. If any child agrees to 'shop' the children, question them closely – perhaps they could persuade them to come along unsuspectingly next morning? Or, after having found out from them where the sea children live, reject their assistance and tell them you won't be needing their help now that you know where to find them.

5. Discuss out of role what has happened. Do we trust the King's adviser? Why not? What is it we don't like about him? Speculate as to why the King of the mainland might want to round up the sea children in his kingdom. What might he do with them? What

Such discussion time is important as it gives the children space to think about what has been happening and what it might all mean. It will also allow any children who decided to betray the sea children to place some distance between themselves and their actions in role.

alternatives are now open to the island children? They cannot possibly attack the soldiers but they can try to warn their friends and, if possible, help them.

The fact that the search for the sea children will not take place until dawn is, of course, a device to give the children space in which they can attempt to pass on a warning – and have an adventure!

6. Split the children into groups of three and ask them to number themselves, 1, 2, 3. Choose one of these numbers as the child who is to represent the fisherman, sitting up late, mending his nets. He is unaware of the presence of the King's men. Then **narrate** the journey that night of the two children sent to warn the sea children, from the village to the fisherman's cottage. At the last minute, they make a noise and are caught by the fisherman who demands that they explain themselves.

You need a large space, such as the hall for this activity. The children need to position themselves as far away from their fisherman as possible. Narrate the journey in hushed tones, building up the atmosphere and adding all the details – how they climb out of their bedroom window at midnight, creep along the shadows of the street, just avoid being seen by a soldier on watch, etc.

7. The children sit in front of the fisherman's chair. Their task is to persuade him that his children are indeed in danger. He, however, is sceptical and is not so readily convinced. Let the **role play** run for a few minutes – it does not necessarily have to be resolved by each group.

While introducing this activity, ask the children to consider reasons as to why the fisherman might be sceptical; perhaps his children have been bullied at school and he thinks this is a trick.

8. Have those children who played the fisherman come and sit in front of you, with the pairs of children sitting behind them. **Question** each fisherman briefly in turn as to what his decision has been or is likely to be. Ask why he found the children either convincing or unconvincing.

This is an opportunity for children to consider how to present themselves to adults, particularly how they should talk to them when they want their arguments to be listened to.

Discuss what possibilities are now open to them to help save the sea children.	
Assessment criteria How well do children respond to the teacher in role as the King's adviser in Activity 4? How plausible/helpful are the children's ideas in terms of plot development in Activities 4 and 8? How well do children enact their respective roles in Activity 7?	

Literacy objectives and related activities

Pupils should be taught: **Fiction and Poetry**	**Examples from work, Week 2**
Writing composition 11. to write own versions of legends, myths and fables, using structures and themes identified in reading;	*Children begin to write their version of the 'The Sea Children', taking care to set the scene clearly. Explore possible openings to the story and perspectives from which it can be told.*
13. to review and edit writing to produce a final form, matched to the needs of an identified reader;	*Children write this story from the beginning as one that will appeal to children of their own age or slightly younger. When finished, it will be given to a child in another class who will return it with a short review.*

Discussion/circle time

1. What reasons do we think the King might have for wishing to be rid of the sea children? How might we argue against these?
2. Why was it important to convince the fisherman of the truth of your story? Have you ever tried to tell a grown-up something true and they wouldn't believe you? Why wouldn't they? How can we get grown-ups to listen to us and take us seriously?

Week 3

Story: The Sea Woman
DRAMA: LESSON THREE

Key moral ideas
- Respecting racial and cultural difference
- Bullying and abuse of power
- Trust and loyalty

Learning objectives in drama
By the end of the lesson, children will have:
- devised and presented a piece of drama with the emphasis on communication through gesture and mime
- articulated the moral themes of the drama through sustained role play

Resources
Walking stick; small leather pouch with coins

Sequence of Activities	*Commentary*
1. **Warm-up** – similar to the warm-up activity in the last session. You may ask the children this time to move between freezes in the form of the sea, using flowing, gentle movements then freezing in rigid, hard shapes.	
2. Recap the drama so far and pose the question – what now? Discuss with children what they *can't* do, i.e. fight the army (there are too many soldiers); hide the children in a house, barn or cave (the soldiers will search them). Tell them the challenge is to use their brains, to outwit rather than outfight the soldiers.	*The children are here challenged to find a solution different from the obvious. Sometimes they decide to call on the mother who brings them seal skins and they go to live with her until it is safe.*
3. Divide the children into groups of five and tell them to decide how the sea children are to be saved and to **act out** their ideas.	*As soon as children have agreed a possible idea, have them work it out on their feet.*

4. After a few minutes, when their ideas are taking shape, ask groups to refine them into a **short play**. To build upon the physical work of the first session, you might ask for this to be done in **mime**. This means actions and movements must be very clear. No miming of speech, however – speech can be included when necessary. These can then be presented under performance conditions.

Mime is suitable here as the escape of the sea children will probably involve more physical than verbal action for children of this age. When the children have performed their work, encourage comment on the clarity of meaning. Solicit praise for particularly satisfying ideas and for skilful examples of mime, movement and expression.

5. Reach some consensus from the plays devised as to how the sea children might have escaped. Explain that the King's adviser was angry, captured the father and brought him in for 'questioning'. Ask for a volunteer and **sculpt** them into an image of the father slumped in a chair, evidently suffering from torture. Ask children to interpret what they have just seen.

Alternatively, model this image yourself and whisper some words, such as 'It doesn't matter what you do to me – you'll never find them.'

6. The island children re-gather in the school hall as they did at the beginning of the drama. **Teacher in role** as the adviser. Point to the father – that is what happens to those who displease the King. You will soon be leaving the island with your men. The sea children have escaped, you realise that. But there's one thing you can't understand. Why did they help them? The father, you can understand, but you offered them gold, the gratitude of a king? Instead they chose to help a group of children who are sub-human. Why? You are going to have to explain this to the King – what are you to say to him?

This is an important exercise. Here you are trying to provoke the children into articulating the values emphasised in the drama – of friendship, loyalty and above all of how wrong it is to label the sea children as sub-human and to persecute them because they are different.

7. Discuss the meaning of the drama with the children. Why was the King wrong to persecute the sea children? Why were the children right to help them? Ask them to speculate on what will happen to the adviser when he tells the King he has failed.	*Here you are encouraging the children to reflect upon the values they have articulated above.*

Assessment criteria

How clearly do the children present their meanings in Activity 4?

What responses do the children make to the adviser in Activity 6?

What understandings do the children show in the concluding discussion?

Discussion/circle time

1. Why were the children prepared to help the sea children escape despite the dangers they might have faced as a consequence? What does it mean to be loyal to friends? Can the class recall any examples of loyalty from their experiences or from true stories they know?

2. How did the King and his adviser misuse their power? What is a tyrant? Why is tyranny and bullying wrong? How did the children stand up to the adviser at the end? How can we stand up to bullies? Can we work together to defeat bullies the way the children did? How, for example, can we do this in school?

Year 6
Macbeth

Source:

'Macbeth' in Leon Garfield's *Shakespeare's Stories*, Gollancz, 1985.

National Literacy Strategy: Year 6 Term 1	**Social and Moral Themes**

Word Level Work
Vocabulary extension
W7
Text Level Work
Fiction and Poetry
• Reading comprehension
  T1; T2; T4; T5;
• Writing composition
  T6; T8; T9; T10
Non-fiction
• Writing composition
  T14; T16; T18
	Friendship
	• qualities we admire
	• trust and loyalty
	Rules
	• law breaking and wrongdoing
	• blame, guilt and feeling sorry
	• intention and responsibility
	Property and Power
	• the difference between power and authority
	• the difference between revenge and justice
	• the consequences of crime
	• victims of crime
	• punishment
	• the qualities of leadership

The story

Unlike the other stories in these schemes of work, Macbeth is a play, one of the greatest and most famous ever written. It would be superfluous to summarise the plot here but there are several versions of the play written in story form with children in mind. The one I recommend that you read to your class by Leon Garfield, as well as being written in a succinct and poetic prose that captures the sinister and dark mood of the play, uses Shakespeare's own words in all of the dialogue. It is therefore an excellent introduction both to the plot and to the language of the play, challenging but accessible for children of this age.

Why this story?

• Its themes of power, corruption, treachery and murder make it one of Shakespeare's darkest works but it is precisely these elements of the tale that can appeal to the imaginations of children of this age.
• There is a clear moral framework to the play. Macbeth's deeds are never morally ambiguous but he himself seems to remain nobler than the sum of his crimes. This can help children begin to think about some complex moral questions. How can a good person become bad? Can a person do bad things but still be good?

- The themes of power, crime and justice carry with them associated ideas such as corruption, guilt, revenge and retribution. These will be common themes in many of the dramas children watch on television. The drama work and, in particular, the discussion work in circle or class time, can provide opportunities for children to explore what they mean.

The drama

The drama is spread over four sessions. The work is intended to draw children into the play and to take them through the workings of its plot, giving them opportunities to speculate, predict and discuss the moral implications of its development as well as devise and perform in a variety of modes. It by no means attempts to present children with a *definitive* reading of the play – such would be impossible. It does, however, present a justifiable reading of it, as the story of Macbeth's moral corruption. In selecting aspects of the play to concentrate on with children, I have chosen those that allow them to explore this as well as the play's supernatural elements. (*Note.* Many of the ideas in the first drama session are drawn from the 1996 booklet in the Young Shakespeare Series, written by Sarah Gordon and Christopher Geelan, entitled simply *Macbeth*. It is published by Buttonhole Press.)

Why this drama?

- It will help children grasp the plot of the play and engage with some of its more complex ideas.
- It concentrates on those aspects of the plot most relevant to Macbeth himself.
- It can help children explore ideas of moral character and moral action within a clear and imaginatively appealing context.
- The performance elements require children to sustain atmospheres and moods that are achievable because they are strong and clearly defined.

Proposed timescale for the work: 5 weeks

This timescale is adaptable but I suggest that the drama lessons take place once a week and that children listen to Garfield's version of the story either in episodes, after each lesson, or soon after the fourth session. You may well decide to use passages from the book or even short passages from the original text in the literacy hour. As presented below, the drama lessons are about 1 hour 15 minutes to – 1 hour 30 minutes each in length and need to take place in the hall. The activities matching the NLS objectives are given en bloc at the end of the chapter with an additional column indicating the proposed week of the project in which the suggested activities take place. Many of you will follow a pattern of weekly work around the one text. If you follow the literacy hour activities as I suggest them here, you will need a more flexible approach – perhaps with one hour a week being devoted to the work on *Macbeth*. If that is impossible or in some way undesirable for you, you might use the Garfield text throughout Week 5 of the literacy hour, with some of the written work extending over into a sixth week if necessary.

As well as reading Garfield's text, you may well find it useful to reread the text of the original play in order to update your own knowledge of the detailed points of plot alluded to throughout this scheme of work.

Week 1	Week 2	Week 3	Week 4	Week 5
Drama: Lesson 1 Discussion Written work *Additional English time* *Circle time* *Literacy hour*	Drama: lesson 2 Discussion Written work *Additional English time* *Circle time* *Literacy hour*	Drama: Lesson 3 Discussion Written work *Additional English time* *Circle time* *Literacy hour*	Drama: Lesson 4 Discussion Written work Read the story *Additional English time* *Circle time* *Literacy hour*	Written work *Literacy hour*

Story: Macbeth
LESSON ONE

Key moral ideas
- Qualities of character we admire
- Qualities of leadership
- Trust and loyalty

Key learning objectives in drama
By the end of the lesson, children will have:
- created dramatic atmosphere through sound collage and choral verse work
- begun to respond to some of the major themes of the play

Resources
Crown for Duncan; sword for Macbeth; atmospheric music (e.g. *Music for Films*, Brian Eno); large sheet of paper and marker pen; scarf for a blindfold; 'letter'

Sequence of Activities	***Commentary***

1. Sit children in a circle and introduce them to the background of the play. It begins on a dark, stormy heath. On one side is Great Birnam Wood, on the other High Dunsinane Hill where the King of Scotland lives in his castle with his two sons, Malcolm and Donalbain. Three mysterious old women also live there and at the beginning of this story, they appear out of the fog and mist, waiting for someone. Divide the children into eight groups and give them a line each from the following (Act I, Scene I):
 	
   'When shall we three meet again?
   In thunder, lightning or in rain?
   When the hurlyburly's done,
   When the battle's lost and won.
   That will be ere the set of sun.
   Where the place?
   Upon the heath.
   There to meet Macbeth.'
	You can entice the children's interest by stressing that it is a story of murder, treachery, darkness and horror as well as one of the greatest plays written in English. Provide some minimal historical background – that it is set in Scotland, long ago, at a time when Scotland still had its own kings. Whenever proper names are introduced you can have children repeat them 'with attitude' – High Dunsinane Hill in a strong voice; Great Birnam Wood in a spooky voice, etc.
	
	 Speak the words from the text in a spooky voice and have children repeat their lines like you. Encourage them to speak them in a loud whisper to evoke atmosphere. During their performance, dim the lights and add the music.

Give children a minute to learn their lines then ask them to perform them as though they were emerging from the fog, standing as they speak.

2. Explain to the children that we shall now have the opportunity to find out about the battle referred to and about this Macbeth from the king himself. As **teacher in role**, deliver a monologue from Duncan, providing the necessary background of the battle and giving details of 'brave Macbeth'.

The details can be obtained from the early scenes of the play and should include his title (Thane of Glamis); his prowess; his nobility of spirit; his love for his wife; the loyalty of his friend, Banquo; the thanks of his king; the admiration and respect of the army.

3. Out of role discuss what the children have found out about Macbeth and ask the question – does he appear to be a good man? In what ways?

You can note these qualities down on paper for later reference.

4. In groups of four or five, have the children compose **still images** to represent the qualities of Macbeth as they have been expressed so far. View and discuss the results.

5. In a circle, tell children that we are to find out why the old women are waiting for Macbeth and what they have to tell him. Choose two children as volunteers to represent Banquo and Macbeth entering on to the stormy heath, Choose three children to stand as you speak the lines:

They can be sculpted into shapes to show how they look/feel as the mist comes down.

    'All hail Macbeth, hail to thee
    Thane of Glamis
    All hail Macbeth, hail to thee
    Thane of Cawdor
    All hail Macbeth that shalt be
    King hereafter.'

Speak these lines strongly and ask the children what they think the witches are telling Macbeth. Inform them that the next activity will explore how this must be making him feel.

6. Play a form of **blindman's buff**. Stand the children in a circle and teach them the line 'All hail Macbeth that shalt be King hereafter'. Blindfold a volunteer to be Macbeth and choose another volunteer who is to move around the circle, taunting him with the line. Macbeth must try to catch him to ask him more. At the end of the game, ask the child who represented Macbeth how he felt. Ask the class to think of what questions Macbeth might want to ask the old women.	*Children in the circle must stand, not sit, for safety reasons.* *The game can be played more than once with different children.* *This can be done in the form of* ***thought tracking*** *while children are still in the circle.*
7. **Story tell** the next part of the play up to the end of Act I. (The old women disappear; the Thane of Ross brings news of Macbeth's elevation to be Thane of Cawdor; the king summons and thanks him and announces that he wishes to stay that very night at Macbeth's castle in Inverness). Hold up the scroll of paper and tell children it is the letter Macbeth wrote to his wife before riding home. What do they think is in it?	*You can encourage children to anticipate Macbeth's temptation to kill the king without giving too much away.* *End the lesson on a note of suspense, with anticipation for the next section.*

Assessment criteria

How successfully do they create and sustain the atmosphere in Activity 1?

How clearly do the children show Macbeth's qualities in action through the still images?

How well do they understand what Macbeth is now considering at the end of the lesson?

Discussion/circle time

1. List the qualities we admire in Macbeth and those we don't, and begin a 'Macbeth popularity poll' by asking the class to award him marks out of ten for overall goodness. After each session, add to the list and rerun the poll. Keep a record each week and use the comparisons as a point of discussion.

2. Do the children have particular heroes, male or female? Discuss the qualities of character they admire in them and compare them with the list we have for Macbeth.

3. Discuss whether they think Macbeth will make a good king from what they know of him so far. Why? What other kinds of leaders can they think of (e.g. head of the school, manager or captain of a sports team)? What qualities make a good leader?

4. Do the children ever take on a role of leadership? When? As the top year in their school, what kind of responsibilities do they have?

5. Should Macbeth trust the old women? Why/why not? Whom do the children trust? Have they any stories about when they had to decide whether to trust someone or not?

6. Should Macbeth be loyal to his king? Why/why not? Has the king done anything to deserve his loyalty?

Story: Macbeth
LESSON TWO

Key moral ideas
- Law breaking and wrongdoing
- Intention and responsibility
- Blame, guilt and feeling sorry

Learning objectives in drama
By the end of the lesson, children will have:
- predicted possibilities in plot and story line
- created and presented clearly a possible version of how Duncan is murdered
- explored the beginnings of Macbeth's moral corruption

Resources
The usual props; two daggers

Sequence of Activities	Commentary
1. Play the game *Assassin* to create a feeling of confusion, isolation, danger. Ask children about the feelings the game creates and ask who in the play they think the assassin will be?	
2. List four or five reasons why Macbeth should kill the king and four or five why he shouldn't. Divide the class into two and have each half choose a reason from the different lists. Create a **conscience alley** as Macbeth approaches Duncan with a dagger. Afterwards, ask the child who represented Macbeth which of the reasons were most persuasive.	*The conscience alley can be staged with eerie music and dimmed lights. A child can stand at the end of the alley as Duncan, with his back to Macbeth. Macbeth can strike with the dagger or drop it, depending on his decision.*

3. In groups of five, children **act out** how they think Duncan was murdered, then rehearse and present a **snapshot** of it. Ask them to include something said by Duncan before he dies to make Macbeth feel guilty and ask the children to make this guilt visible – through facial expression, gesture, etc. These are then presented in sequence and discussed.

Ask children to consider questions such as: How was the murder committed? Who did the deed? What about the king's guards? And how was it planned so the blame was cast on someone else? And did it all go smoothly? These can be written on a large sheet of paper and displayed.

4. Sit the children in a circle. Choose one of the snapshots to be performed again and hold the final image for a short time. Relate how Macbeth thought he heard voices accusing him from the darkness – what might they have said? Write down some suggestions, ask children to choose one, then show the final image again with a **voice collage** echoing over it. Join in, whispering intermittently Shakespeare's words: 'Sleep no more, Macbeth doth murder sleep'. Afterwards, discuss what the children understand by these particular words.

Add music if possible.

5. Choose the final image of another group's work and add two daggers to it, placing them on the bodies of the guards. **Narrate** the following action. The children **act out** the story as you narrate it. 'After the deed was committed, the noble lord Macduff arrived to awaken the king early. Macbeth led him to the king's chamber, then waited outside while Macduff entered

Choose the image that comes closest to Shakespeare's own version of Duncan's murder.
Add the roles of Lennox and Macduff and ensure the children know who they are. Ensure the circle is large enough to have spaces representing the inside and the outside of the king's chamber. The narration emphasises action. The children simply act what you relate and alone. On seeing

the dead king, Macduff screamed "Oh horror, horror, horror" and ran out of the room. Macbeth asked "What is't you say?" Macduff turned to him "Approach the chamber and see." Macbeth entered with Lennox. Lennox gazed in horror at the blood soaked corpse of the king. Macbeth pretended to gaze in horror and then pointed to the guards. Lennox could see that they were covered in blood. With a roar, Macbeth leapt on one of them and plunged the dagger into his heart. Then he leapt on to the other and did the same. Pretending to weep, he ran down into the courtyard, where all were gathering.'

6. Ask if Macduff might have any suspicions. What questions might he now want to ask Macbeth and how might Macbeth answer them? Children **hot seat** Macbeth who must remain completely calm and try to convince everyone that he had nothing to do with the murder.

repeat any words you say in the manner in which you say them.

Ask the children afterwards how they think the guards came to be sleeping and covered in blood. Then discuss the differences/similarities between the children's versions of Duncan's murder and Shakespeare's.

*This hot seating can be carried out in a number of ways: as a whole class, with teacher in role, a child in role, or three or four children in **collective role** as Macbeth. After this sequence of whole-class work, however, it is perhaps best done in small groups, with one child as Macbeth in each group.*

Assessment criteria

What reasons do the children suggest as to why Macbeth should or should not commit the murder?

Do they appreciate his subsequent sense of guilt? (Activity 5)

How successfully do the groups' versions of the murder of Duncan meet the criteria you set for them in Activity 4? Are the presentations clearly understandable?

Discussion/circle time

1. Why is the killing of Duncan such an appalling murder? List the reasons (e.g. Duncan was Macbeth's guest; Duncan was asleep; Duncan was his king) and ask children to try and place them in what they consider the order of importance.
2. Introduce concepts such as 'treacherous' and add them to the list of Macbeth's qualities.
3. What do we mean when we say someone is *guilty* of a crime or of doing something wrong? What do we mean when we say we *feel* guilty about doing something? Have the children ever done something that they regretted afterwards, even though they weren't punished for it? Why did they feel bad?

Story: Macbeth
LESSON THREE

Key moral ideas
- Responsibility and wrongdoing
- Trust and loyalty
- Power and corruption

Learning objectives in drama
By the end of the lesson, children will have:
- sequenced events from a narrative in the form of a dramatic framework
- improvised, rehearsed and presented a scene with special attention to the use of space (proxemics) and voice

Resources
The usual props

Sequence of Activities	Commentary
1. Recap the story so far. Then do some **story telling** in role. As one of Macbeth's chatty but naïve servants, relate the plot from the flight of Malcolm and Donalbain (Act II, Scene IV) to the appearance of Banquo's ghost and the break-up of the banquet (Act III, Scene V). Before beginning, explain to the children that this character witnessed things he or she didn't understand and that their challenge is to figure out what really happened and provide the missing details.	*Relate only those things you could have heard about or seen for yourself as a servant and feel free to add details that include you at the scene – brushing the yard when two shady looking characters knocked at the gates; serving at the banquet etc. Of course, you know nothing of the ghost, only Macbeth's reactions. You know that Banquo's body was found murdered next day but make no connection etc.*
2. Discuss with the children what they think happened, then list this section of the plot in the form of a dramatic skeleton, e.g. Macbeth talks to Banquo and Banquo exits; the two murderers enter and talk with Macbeth, etc.	*Do this on two large sheets of paper in the form of two scenes, to lead into the next exercise. Have them displayed so that the groups can consult them as necessary.*

3. In groups of five or six, children are now set the task of **acting out** the story told by the servant, with the missing details (dialogue with murderers, apparition of ghost, etc.) included. Groups will concentrate on either (Scene I), the story up to the dispatch of the murderers to kill Banquo; or (Scene II), the events at the feast up to the dispersal of the guests. In (I) the characters are: Macbeth, Banquo, servant, two murderers; and in (II) Macbeth, Lady Macbeth, Banquo's ghost, murderer, guest and servant. These are refined for **performance**. Ensure each group receives adequate help/guidance.

Instruct the children to think carefully about their use of dramatic space and voice. Where should Macbeth and the murderers stand so that the audience hears them but understands that the servant doesn't, for example? How should he talk to the murderers, to Banquo, to his guests? Rather than as playlets, the children can prepare and present their ideas as a sequence of three moving snippets with two or three lines of dialogue in each – this will give them time to concentrate on the stage picture and the use of voice.

4. Before presenting these in uninterrupted sequence, ask the children to pick out at least one thing from what they are about to see that they find particularly impressive. After the presentations, share these points of praise and negotiate choosing one of the groups to look at in more detail. Analyse with the class one or two instances of use of space and/or dialogue and seek out possible alternatives. 'Let's see what it would be like if the ghost sat with his back to Macbeth. Is that an improvement, do you think? Why?' etc.

If a group finishes well before others are ready you can stop the class and have them watch, praise, then interrogate this piece of work. They can then return to their groups with the instruction to apply what they have learned to their own work. Members of the group that has finished can be split up and shared around the class to act as 'outside eyes' – to watch in silence as different groups work but to be available to offer advice or comment if called upon.

5. Finish the lesson on a note of anticipation; how are Macbeth's schemes going wrong? Is the bloodshed over? What other crimes may he have in mind?

Assessment criteria
How well can the children turn the narrative story into a framework for drama in Activity 2 or do they rely heavily on the teacher's input?
How well do the children use space and voice in Activity 3?

Discussion/circle time

1. Add words like 'mistrustful' 'jealous' 'bloodthirsty' 'brutal' to our list of qualities. Why is Macbeth becoming like this?
2. Discuss whether getting involved in crime or wrongdoing can lead into further crime or wrongdoing.
3. Why does Macbeth cease to be friendly with Banquo? What kinds of things lead the children to fall out with their friends? Have they any stories to share? Did they make up? How?
4. Do they think Banquo's ghost actually exists or is Macbeth imagining it? If he is imagining it, why? Do children believe in ghosts? Why has Banquo's ghost returned to Macbeth? Do they have any stories to share of people they know who say they have seen a ghost? Do they believe them?

Story: Macbeth
LESSON FOUR

Key moral ideas
● Justice and revenge
● Punishment and retribution

Learning objectives in drama
By the end of the lesson, children will have:
● created and sustained dramatic atmosphere through voice and movement
● speculated on and represented what they feel would be a fitting dramatic conclusion to the story

Resources
Usual props; blindfold; copies of individual lines to hand out to groups (see Activity 2)

Sequence of Activities	*Commentary*
1. **Warm-up**. Lead the children through some slow motion effort exercises. On the spot, they push, pull, twist in different directions and at different levels. Then use similar sorts of movement to travel slowly through space.	*Add sinister music when they begin to travel and narrate: 'You're a moving shadow, a ghost, mysterious and threatening, forever changing your shape as you move through space', etc.*
2. Tell of Macbeth's decision to go back to the weird sisters – why might he have done that? Divide children into six groups and share the following lines between them, one for each group: ● *Macbeth, Macbeth, beware Macduff, beware the Thane of Fife* ● *Macbeth, Macbeth, be bloody, bold and resolute, for none of woman born shall harm Macbeth* ● *Macbeth shall never vanquished be until Great Birnam Wood to High Dunsinane Hill shall come against him*	*These lines are taken from Act IV, Scene I. It will help if you have prepared two copies of each line, written in large, to distribute to the groups. Read each in turn and have the groups follow your reading. Discuss the literal meaning of each. Have groups experiment with reading them in ways that create an eerie atmosphere. Then set them a deadline of two minutes to learn them off by heart, if they can. Alternatively, children may learn phrases from the line.*

3. Divide the class in half, three groups in each, with each line represented by a group in each half. Sit half of the class close together in the centre of the room with the other groups encircling them. Tell the children in the centre to close their eyes while the other half **perform** their lines in sequence in an eerie way. Add atmospheric music. Repeat with each half swapping places.

You can conduct this exercise, like a **sound collage***, having children repeat their lines as you point to them, controlling volume, having lines overlap, etc. It can be very effective if performers move around as they speak. At the end of the exercise, ask the children in the centre which phrases stuck out for them and why.*

4. What are the old women telling Macbeth? If they are right, what should Macbeth be thinking now? Why did we present them in such a scarey way?

This can get children to think of how we have created suspense. They can sense that Macbeth shouldn't trust the witches, that there must be a catch.

5. **Storytell** the main events of the plot between Act IV, Scene II to Act V, Scene V. These include: Macduff's flight to England; the murder of his family; Macduff's meeting with Malcolm and their raising an army to fight Macbeth; the decline and death of Lady Macbeth; Macbeth's isolation; Macduff's encampment in Birnam Wood and his need for camouflage. Encourage children to speculate how Birnam Wood might indeed travel to Dunsinane without any supernatural meaning.

This is a large section of the play but there is much in the text – for example the long scene between Macduff and Malcolm – that might easily lose the interest of the children. Garfield's text can be a very useful guide here to your tone and selection of detail.

6. List the different people Macbeth has murdered. What would the different ghosts he has made accuse him of? Write down suggestions alongside each and display them.

7. Form children into groups of five or six. They are to imagine a nightmare vision Macbeth has of Birnam Wood coming to Dunsinane in the form of these ghosts closing in on him. One child takes on the role of Macbeth, the others use the movement work developed in *Activity 1* as a basis to represent the approach of the ghosts. Ask each ghost to choose one of the accusations to whisper at Macbeth, getting louder as they approach. Create a clear, closing image. **Rehearse and perform in sequence**.	*Ensure that each group's working space is clearly defined.* *To help create a sense of menace, suggest that the ghosts keep their eyes focused on Macbeth through-out.* *Once again, atmospheric music can greatly add to the effect of the performance.*
8. Ask children to choose a partner, find their own space and label one another A and B. Then **storytell** the rest of the plot, of how the castle is stormed and of how Macbeth and Macduff come face to face in battle. On approaching Macbeth, Macduff informs him that he is, indeed, not of woman born. **Sculpt** the two facing each other and have children **thought track** what each might be thinking in turn. Explain that this is the climax of the play. In pairs, children **rehearse and perform** a slow-motion fight to illustrate how it ends and who they think will win, Macbeth or Macduff.	*These are best viewed with three or four pairs performing at once. When they have finished, points to praise can be sought and you can ask groups to show by raising their hands whether they decided Macbeth or Macduff ought to win. These decisions can be discussed now or in class later.*
9. Children form **a line of allegiance**. The point on the extreme right is for those who believe passionately that Macbeth *deserved* to die; on the extreme left for those who believe passionately he deserved to live.	*This can lead into a useful discussion as to how and why Macbeth causes a mixture of feelings in us; how part of us still likes and pities him despite the horrific crimes he is responsible for.*

Children can place themselves at any point along the line. The same exercise can then be repeated to the question as to whether they *wanted* Macbeth to live or die.	

Assessment criteria
How well do the children use their voices and bodies to present menace in Activities 3 and 7?
How effectively do their images in Activity 7 make use of space?
Are they sensitive to the logic of the play in Activity 8?
How aware are they of the nature of Macbeth's crimes and do they retain any ambiguity of feeling toward him as a human being?

Discussion/circle time/further activities

1. At the end of the play, did the children retain any sympathy for Macbeth, despite his crimes? If so, why? If not, why not?
2. At the end of the play, has justice been done? What do we mean by that?
3. Which characters can be said to have had their revenge on Macbeth? What do we mean by 'revenge'? Is it a good or a bad thing? Have the children any stories about when they have taken their revenge against someone? Or when someone has taken their revenge on them?
4. What do the children think should be written on Macbeth's tombstone? Can they write two or four lines in verse by way of an epitaph?

Literacy objectives and related activities

Pupils should be taught: **Word Level Work: Vocabulary extension**	Week	*Examples from this chapter*
7. to understand how words and expressions have changed over time, e.g. old verb endings *-st* and *-th* and how some words have fallen out of use, e.g. *yonder, thither;*	1	*Children list such words from examples of dialogue in the Garfield text and/or from short extracts from the original play. Next to each they provide a modern alternative.*

Text Level Work: Fiction and poetry **Reading comprehension** 1. to compare or evaluate a novel or play in print and the film/TV version, e.g. treatment of the plot and characters, the differences in the two forms, e.g. in seeing the setting, in losing the narrator;	4	*Children watch the version of 'Macbeth' from the Animated Tales of Shakespeare and compare it with the written text by Garfield.*
2. to articulate personal responses to literature, identifying why and how a text affects the reader;	1–4	*Children are regularly asked to make such comments on work in the drama sessions and circle time.*
4. to be familiar with the work of some established authors, to know what is special about their work. . .;	1	*Children can be introduced to the range of Shakespeare's plays, to posters of particular productions, to the role of the Royal Shakespeare Company and its theatres in Stratford and London. The class can discuss what it knows of filmed versions of his plays (e.g. 'Romeo and Juliet').*
5. to contribute constructively to shared discussion about literature responding to and building on the views of others;	1–4	*Much of the discussion in drama and circle time, particularly when focussed on the character and deeds of Macbeth.*
Writing composition 6. to manipulate narrative perspective by writing in the voice and style of a text;	3	*Children change the perspective of the servant's story (Drama: Lesson 3) when devising a framework for their scene. They present this in what they perceive to be Shakespeare's style.*

8. to summarise a passage, chapter or text in a specified number of words;	2	*After the second drama session, children write a summary of the murder of Duncan and the discovery of his body in no more than 100 words.*
9. to prepare a short section of a story as a script, e.g. using stage directions, location/setting;	3	*Children write scripts for the scenes they devised for Macbeth with Banquo's murderers and the appearance of Banquo's ghost at the banquet.*
10. to write own poems experimenting with active verbs and personification; produce revised poems for reading aloud individually;	2, 4	*Children write and read out poems written in the voice of the dagger that slew Duncan and the guards; or on the relentless march of the ghosts of Birnam Wood.*
Non-fiction **Writing composition** 14. to develop the skills of bio-graphical and autobiographical writing in role, adopting distinctive voices, e.g. of historical characters through, for example, describing a person from different perspec-tives such as a police report, news-paper obituary;	2–4	*Write a police report on one of Banquo's murderers; an obituary for Duncan, Banquo, Macbeth or Lady Macbeth.*
16. to use the styles and conventions of journalism to report on e.g. real or imagined events;	5	*Children look at the types of texts in their local newspaper (stories, features, ads, etc) and write a variety of articles for a class version of the 'Dunsinane Echo'. These are based on aspects of the play, e.g. Lead story 'King dies in mysterious circumstances'; Feature 'A ramble through Birnam Wood'; Horoscope by Weird Sister;*

		Today's weather – storm, mist, possibility of severely disturbed horses, etc; *Situations Vacant – throne of Scotland; fourth sister needed – must be weird;* *Missing persons 'Fleance, last seen . . .';* *Small ads – spot remover, will rid your hands of unwanted blood stains.*
18. to use ICT to plan, revise, edit writing to improve accuracy and conciseness and to bring it to publication standard, e.g. through compiling a class newspaper, paying attention to accuracy, layout and presentation;	5	*See above.*

Chapter 2

Planning for moral education through drama

Positioning drama in the moral education curriculum

In your school, the social and moral education of children will take place in a number of ways and much of this will be across or even beyond the curriculum. There will be some sort of instruction in moral codes and values, in what should be understood as right and wrong. Children will also be encouraged to develop particular habits and attitudes, to show consideration for one another for example, and to demonstrate qualities such as honesty and responsibility. They will also be encouraged to think of how their actions can be helpful or hurtful to those around them and to consider what qualities they admire in others and why. This kind of 'training' and 'instruction' of children, although central to a school's moral education programme, is only part of it. Teaching about moral codes or rules might take place in an RE lesson or an assembly and children will be encouraged to show agreed, desirable patterns of behaviour as part of the ethos of the school as a whole. But, in order to develop into independent moral agents, capable of making their own moral judgements when faced with complex and difficult decisions, children need to develop imaginative and emotional qualities that can help them think through difficult moral dilemmas; understand the needs and feelings of others; and develop a language to help them discuss issues of 'good' and 'bad' character, 'right' and 'wrong' action.

As we explored in the Introduction, there are a number of ways in which stories can be harnessed for the purposes of moral education, sometimes with a closed agenda, suggesting what a course of action or a way of living one's life ought to be, but sometimes with a more open agenda, where the difficulties, the ups and downs of experience, are emphasised. If the former type of story is a kind of *instruction* in moral behaviour, the latter is more of an *induction* into a broader consideration of the moral life as something complex and seldom simple. Such stories help children develop those imaginative qualities needed for them to think their way through situations where rules on their own are insufficient or inapplicable. Very importantly, both kinds of stories introduce children to the kind of concepts we might call *virtues* and *vices*, those qualities of character that are recognisable in actions performed in particular contexts;

courage, compassion, loyalty, for example, or cowardice, unkindness and fickleness. But if those stories that try to instruct children in the virtues portray role models for emulation, those that attempt to induct them into thinking conceptually about the virtues regard them as problematic and unfixed. They pose and explore questions about, for example, courage and loyalty rather than offering illustrative blueprints. In this way, the moral life is conveyed as one where the question 'how should I live?' must constantly be asked so that we continue to re-evaluate the social effects of our actions.

Drama, being both social and active by nature and centred around stories, can contribute to both aspects of a primary school's moral curriculum, those involved with the development of positive moral attitudes and behaviour – of care and responsibility, for example – and those that endeavour to introduce children into the conceptual language of moral thinking and develop their imaginative appreciation of the social needs of others. It can use stories to help develop certain moral values and attitudes, certainly; but it can also, very effectively, help children think, feel and ask questions about moral issues that are as complex as they are fundamental to being human. The rest of this chapter will attempt to explain and illustrate how drama can do this, with specific reference to examples drawn from the six drama projects described in the previous chapter. In it I will analyse those aspects of drama that make it well-placed to assist the moral education of children, beginning with the unique way in which stories are experienced through drama, through physical enactment.

The moral power of enacted narrative

In schools, most stories are either read or told; in either case, the medium is words. In drama, words are of course important but they are complemented by a variety of visual and aural signs. The people in the stories are visible and audible; we see how they look and how they act and hear what they say and how they say it. They might be wearing or holding something significant – a hat, an old jacket, a letter, a stick – or they might be sitting in silence as someone else speaks to them or about them or while other sounds can be heard – music, or voices off. These visual and aural signs carry meanings which are both literal and symbolic and which gain added power by operating in both fields of meaning at once.

Objects

In a play, a letter on a table is more than just a communication. If the story is about marital betrayal it could be from a lover, signifying the infidelity of one of the partners or from a blackmailer, signifying their sense of guilt. In both cases we can see that the symbolic meanings carry with them a *moral charge* and, in good drama, this moral charge can be made all the more potent by the sensorial impact of our *seeing* the letter there and *listening*, for example, to the good-natured but ironic chat of the innocent partner. Even the most everyday objects can in this way become symbolically charged when used effectively in drama, resonating a moral force they seldom carry in everyday life.

Examples
The Frog Prince, Lesson 2. The **golden ball** represents those objects to which children are emotionally attached, irrespective of their economic value.
Tinker Jim, Lesson 1. The **tin of catfood** represents the vicar's selfishness and lack of charity.
Sho, Lesson 3. **The silver coins** represent the refuse collector's willingness to exploit other people's problems for his own gain.
Sweet Clara. The **quilt** symbolises what the slaves can achieve as a community, their communal endeavour to find freedom and happiness.
The Sea Woman, Lesson 1. As both skin and net, the **netting** symbolises how the Sea Woman is trapped by having her identity – that which makes her different – denied her by the fisherman's selfish possession of her.
Macbeth, Lesson 2. Macbeth is hot-seated on his throne after the murder and lies his way calmly out of any awkward questions. Here the ordinary **chair** represents a throne that, in this situation, symbolises the arrogance of power. Later, in Lesson 4, a group of children created a similar image as Macbeth was approached by the ghosts of Birnam Wood. Here the throne carried a different meaning – the lonely, corrupt and ultimately ruinous achievements of his ambition.

It is important at this point to differentiate the term *moral* from the term *moralistic.* The moral charge in such symbols is not there to teach or reinforce ideas of right and wrong; the objects carry moral weight inasmuch as they encapsulate particular moral ideas about certain human actions in specific situations. The understandings they make available to children do not necessarily need to be analysed; but they do need to be felt and they can animate some powerful discussion.

Objects in space

Objects in drama are not seen in isolation; they exist in space and their position in that space can add suggestively to their symbolic, moral meanings.

Example
Sweet Clara, Lesson 1. The **North Star**, represented by the light of a torch high on the wall of a darkened room. A light shining in the darkness; a cultural reference to the star of Bethlehem, perhaps, promising a new era; a potent symbol of hope. These meanings are best apprehended, however, by adding the **image of Aunt Rachel**, standing some distance away, gazing up at it.

The moral power children are able to draw from such images can be reflected in the comments they make through **thought tracking**. One group of children immediately grasped the significance of this image as one of hope, with comments like 'I hope they get away safely', 'I hope they're as lucky as Clara'; 'I hope I get away too some day'; 'I hope I see Clara again'.

Sound

The addition of sound, particularly music, to visual images is very common in film and TV drama but less so in classrooms. And yet it can very effectively intensify children's ability to grasp the significance of a dramatic image and feel the emotional power of its moral charge. We need to remember, too, that words carry more than sense; they, too, possess potential musical qualities, exploited in particular in poetry and song, but equally available for drama teachers to make use of.

Examples
Sho, Lesson 1. The children use their voices to emphasise the contrast between the destructive nature of the demons and the healing qualities of Sho.
Macbeth, Lesson 2. Children whisper contradictory advice in the form of a **conscience alley** as Macbeth approaches Duncan. Here their comments as to why Macbeth should or shouldn't kill the king emphasise the oppositional pull between his sense of morality and the force of his ambition. If the lights are dimmed and eerie music is layered over the image, the dark nature of the act he is considering is emphasised and the moral stake of this decision is heightened.
Sea Woman, Lesson 1. The **sound collage** that surrounds the fisherman as he stands alone in the sea after the Sea Woman has left him and his children underlines his moral responsibility for the situation he and his children now find themselves in. At the same time, appropriate music, playing softly, will add a feeling of moral ambivalence to the image by intensifying the pathos of the moment, moving the children to feel sorry for him. The significance of such ambivalence is discussed below.

Movement and stillness

If objects convey moral power when in a dramatic space, then people do so even more, both through movement and through stillness. Working with stillness in drama can be doubly beneficial for young children as it can allow them to portray a moral idea with simplicity whilst providing others with the time to examine and respond to it. The use of the **still image** is a simple but powerful way to enable this but stillness can also be incorporated inside the action of a drama with the same potential to stimulate a moral response.

Examples

Sho, Lesson 2. Through violent and contorted movements the children evoke the evil and destructive power of the demons.

Macbeth, Lesson 4. The slow but relentless approach of the ghosts of Birnam Wood represents the inevitable defeat of Macbeth and revenge for the evil he has perpetrated.

The Sea Woman. When children create a **still image** of the worst moment in the story for the Sea Woman, they are being asked to consider images of suffering in ways that can help them empathise with her. In order to articulate this understanding, they must speculate on how the characters of the fisherman and the Sea Woman relate to one another in space, by commenting on their respective levels, their postures, their gestures and their facial expressions.

The Sea Woman, Lesson 3. A child sits in role as the fisherman, slumped in a chair, now himself a victim, of torture and of tyranny. The presence of this image can do much to energise the children in their dialogue with the King's adviser and their refutation of the King's racist values.

Sweet Clara, Lesson 2. When the doctor has the injured slave trapped in his house, a child sits alone and still, some distance from his classmates. This literal separation in space, emphasising his isolation, represents visually the threat now posed to the promise made by the slaves to stick together at all costs.

Teacher in role

In our consideration of the physical representation of people in drama, of central importance is the teacher's use of teacher in role. By the characters the teacher chooses to play and the way he or she chooses to play them, children can be guided into articulating **unambiguous moral responses**.

When a character is more rounded, or when their actions are more contradictory, a more complex response is called for. Children can feel warmth towards a character while, at the same time, they judge his or her actions to be wrong. Here they are feeling an **ambivalent moral response**. In general, the older children become, the more we should attempt to engage them with more ambivalent and difficult moral responses. Exploring with children the very human, contradictory feelings such characters arouse within us is one of the most important ways we can use drama to initiate them into the more open-ended, 'inductive' curriculum, to complement their moral instruction.

Examples

The Frog Prince, Lesson 3. The princess's haughtiness emphasises that the children's sympathies lie with the Frog Prince, not with her.

Tinker Jim. The vicar and Lady Higg are quite clearly **types**, that is to say, two-dimensional characters depicting and representing moral failings that the children can readily recognise and condemn. This kind of character is common in pantomime. Here, the one represents a lack of charity (all the more pointed as he is a religious minister), the other out-and-out selfishness.

Sweet Clara, Lesson 2. The doctor at first appears to be a true friend to the slaves but then reveals himself to be a false friend, insisting on payment at the expense of a slave's freedom. His actions pose certain moral questions. Should human beings ever be regarded as economic chattels? When should someone else's problems become my problems? Should we help others, regardless of what they can do for us? These questions become the subject of the ensuing dialogue between the doctor and the slaves but, in their role as slaves, the children's response to the doctor's actions remains unambiguous; he is wrong to act as he does. The challenge for them is to articulate why and to do something about it.

Examples

Tinker Jim, Lesson 3. The children know that Jim shouldn't steal but they don't like Lady Higg (whom he steals from) and they do like him. They also understand *why* he steals from her. The moral thrust therefore centres around issues of justice. How wrong do the children judge his actions to be? Should he be punished? How? Is there anything we can do so that he will not have to steal in future?

Sho, Lesson 3. Although the refuse collector is quite unambiguous in the first activity, his willingness to accept the Emperor's rule of law and his subsequent request for the children's help can work to change their attitude towards him.

Macbeth. Moral ambivalence is, in a far more complex way, at the heart of our response to Macbeth as a character, a man who embodies virtues we admire even as he is responsible for the most appalling crimes. This is made evident by the contradictory feelings many children will own to at the end of Lesson 4.

'Acting responsibly'

Those teachers who have worked in role with children will know how powerful its effects can be; and, as we have seen, your choice of role will serve to prompt different responses from your class. With younger children, in particular, you may well be concerned that the actions they take within the drama should be 'virtuous' as opposed to 'vicious'. The most straightforward way to ensure this is to take on the role of someone whom the children will sympathise with and who will need their help. Children at Key Stage 1, in particular, will almost always readily identify with such characters and be willing to help them. In helping someone who in the fictional world is in some way more disadvantaged than themselves, children will demonstrate such virtues as concern for others; generosity of spirit; compassion; and a belief in social justice.

Examples
The Frog Prince, Lesson 2. The frog is too small to hop on to the witch's window so the children look in for him. They also capture the witch's book of spells for him and show the princess how easy it is to kiss him!
Tinker Jim, Lesson 2. Jim is too disheartened to go and ask Lady Higg for food so the children go on his behalf.
Sho, Lesson 3. In role as the villagers, the children have to enforce the new, just law of the Emperor and explain *why* it is just to the refuse collector.

It would, of course, be naive to expect children to transfer these modes of behaviour directly into their everyday lives. There is always a distance between the person I am when acting or in role and the person I am in everyday life. This does not, however, deny the validity of having children take on such roles for there is always something of me, of my 'self', in this 'other' I am pretending to be. Drawing from my knowledge of the world and my own experience I enter into a 'third space', one that can help me make connections between my sense of self and how it differs from or is similar to or connects me with others. Through dramas such as these, albeit in fictional situations, children practise the virtues that the school tries to encourage. In this way they are given the opportunity to explore ethical actions within particular contexts. It may be impossible to know the residual, internal effects that dramatising such actions will leave with children; but, at the very least, they provide new, communally shared stories to build up their moral reference points, stories that the teacher can draw upon in later discussion.

Children in upper KS2 usually need more subtle approaches when being enrolled into roles that carry with them a moral dimension. A common strategy is to enrol them as experts such as detectives or scientists as these roles bring with them certain ethical codes of practice that children are familiar with from their social experience and from their viewing of TV drama. Another good strategy is to pit the children in role against an obviously pernicious force of authority whose intentions they will enjoy subverting.

Example
Sea Woman, Lesson 2. It will evidently be much more fun for the children to subvert the evil intentions of the King's adviser than to allow him to win. Here their role as helpers is given the added spice of an adventure story, where they are also called upon to demonstrate the virtues of courage and loyalty.

Of course, children will not always take on such 'virtuous' roles in their drama or in their play. Part of the fun of the work can lie in the freedom it grants them to take on other identities and to play at being villainous or grotesquely evil.

Examples

The Frog Prince, Lesson 2. Children mould a volunteer into the most evil looking witch they can imagine.

Tinker Jim, Lessons 2 and 3. As Lady Higg or the vicar, children can play at being as smug and as selfish as possible.

Sho, Lessons 1 and 2. Children have the chance to enjoy representing the monstrous behaviour of the demons.

Macbeth. Throughout the drama work children have great fun depicting acts of evil, horror and murder.

Teachers sometimes worry about this aspect of drama and, even if they don't, they might certainly think twice before claiming any moral learning for it. We must not forget, however, that in stories such as Macbeth evil acts do not exist within a moral vacuum; they are understood as evil and ultimately, justice is seen to be done and punishment meted out. In a psychological sense, children may or may not be playing out their fears and anxieties in such work but, in a social sense, they can be acknowledging what they know to be right by playing out actions they understand to be wrong. With older children we can begin to explore *why* people, even those with qualities we admire such as Macbeth, commit acts we judge to be bad. But the aspect of fun, of playing with horror and the grotesque, should remind us that, at base, drama remains a playful art form and it is to a consideration of the moral learning that *drama as game* can offer that we turn to next. First of all, I offer the following points to assist you with your planning, drawn from the chapter so far.

Planning points

- Consider where and how you can use symbolic objects in your drama lessons and what possible meanings they might convey in the form of a moral charge.
- Consider carefully your use of space and how objects and/or people can be positioned within it to heighten particular moral tensions.
- Be aware of the moral dimensions of the roles you take on yourself. Are they straightforward 'types' or representative of more complex characters? In either case, what is their moral significance?
- When choosing roles for the children, consider the possibilities for ethical or unethical action that they can explore through them.
- Can music or other uses of sound deepen children's receptiveness towards particular moral tensions?
- Build in time for reflection and/or discussion of the moral points that arise either inside or outside the drama.

Games, rules and drama

Games and rules

Young children can learn many things that have a bearing on their social and moral development through playing games. Games take place in a social space that allows children to connect with and relate to others. They help them learn about turn-taking, about fairness, about living with disappointment as well as success, about seeing difficulties as a challenge. They can encourage feelings of mutuality and trust. Above all, they can teach children to appreciate that rules are a necessary and enabling feature of social encounters; that we can get on with one another with agreed rules more easily than we can without them. They can also teach them about patience and self-discipline as both are called for if a game is to be enjoyed properly: a football match or a game of snakes and ladders is no fun if it lasts only for two minutes or if someone persistently cheats.

There is something of a chicken and egg relationship between social learning and games; children need to demonstrate social skills in order to play them and can improve these skills *through* playing them. And many of these skills can develop children's moral attitudes, teaching them to accept negotiated agreement; to respect group endeavour; to stick to certain principles of social conduct; and to demonstrate self-discipline. Games foreground the need for such attitudes and provide structures that allow for quick and visible rewards when they are demonstrated.

It is a good idea to build one or two games into the structure of your lessons, either as warm-ups or as part of the story line. Some games can have an explicitly moral content.

Examples
My treasured possession, The Frog Prince, Lesson 1. Encourages children to consider that there is more to value than monetary worth.
'One good thing about. . .' Sweet Clara, Lesson 2. Encourages children to give and receive praise.

However, it is not principally through their content but through their structures – that is, through their rules – that games can encourage the development of specific moral attitudes.

Examples
Circle games, Year 1. These teach turn-taking and establish a sense of equality, that everyone has the right to be heard.
Tag games such as 'Tinker Jim chasing the chickens'. As a warm-up, children have to work hard to free those classmates who have been caught and they must accept it when they are caught themselves. The teacher can ask children to count the number of classmates they free to make it an important feature of the game.
Tinker Jim and the Butler, Lesson 3. Encourages self-discipline as everyone must be still and quiet; and patience on the part of the children playing Jim and the Butler.

This emphasis on structure rather than content is important as it helps us understand that there can be social and moral learning independent of the transgressive nature of a game's apparent subject. A child playing *Tinker Jim chasing the chickens* is in no greater danger of learning that stealing is fun than a child playing *Assassin* is of learning how to commit murder by stealth!

Drama and rules

Games and drama are different kinds of play activity but they both operate through rules. In drama the rules tend to be implicit rather than explicit but teachers can still contract in different kinds of positive behaviour to help guide the activities in a drama lesson.

Examples

All year groups. Whenever a group's work is viewed by the class, it is understood that both teacher and children will only make positive comments. This fosters trust between teacher and children and between the children themselves.

Macbeth, Lesson 3. One group works quickly and demonstrates to the class what it has done. As the rest of the children complete their pieces, the members of this group are attached to different groups as 'outside eyes'. They are instructed to observe and only offer advice when asked for by the group members. This ensures that criticism is focused on what the group sees as important and is only voiced when asked for.

Shared performance. The Sea Woman, Lesson 3, and *Macbeth, Lesson 3*, contain examples of the whole class creating short pieces of theatre in groups then sharing them with one another. These are presented, from first to last, under the rules of performance, with the only talk and movement coming from whichever group happens to be performing at the time. The group discipline here is presented both as a challenge and as an act of respect, for their own and their classmates' work. It can quickly reward children by helping them feel the greater, dramatic enjoyment such discipline brings to the experience of actor and audience.

The rules of drama are perhaps best described as *conventions* for, if rules carry the connotation of something fixed and imposed, then conventions suggest group agreement and negotiation. One thing that children can learn from drama, that they do not learn so readily from games, is how to negotiate rules.

Examples

The Frog Prince. The class and the teacher together decide how they might best represent the witch in her cottage; and how they all need to behave to ensure she does not see them.

Sho, Lesson 3. The children negotiate with the Emperor the wording for the new law that will forbid the dumping of nightmares and other nasty things into the sea.

Sweet Clara, Lesson 1. The children in groups decide what food each is to take with them so that they will have a variety to share on the journey.

The Sea Woman, Lesson 2. Children are asked to volunteer suggestions as to how the images ought to be sequenced for the performance.

The game of drama

Another key feature that distinguishes sporting games, in particular, from drama is the fact that, unlike soccer or netball, drama takes its content directly from the social world. But in the process of mirroring social encounters, the game-like quality still pervades how these encounters are represented. In particular, just as a game of chess or football is more engaging for the participants if victory is not too easy, the various encounters children face in a fictional drama world will captivate them more if the tensions are sustained and the resolutions delayed. This is important as it helps us understand how children can enjoy the deferment of pleasure as opposed to immediate gratification, and how drama can help them learn to enjoy the challenge of something difficult.

Examples

Sweet Clara, Lessons 2 and 3. As slaves the children want to reach the Ohio River at all costs, but as participants in a drama, they do not want to get there without facing genuine difficulties that they must work hard at to overcome.

The Sea Woman, Lesson 2. The children must attempt to persuade the fisherman that there is a genuine danger; the child in role as the fisherman must make the children work hard to gain his trust.

Macbeth, Lesson 2. Children attempt to expose Macbeth's lies as they hot seat him. He in his turn tries to remain calm and king-like.

This last example returns us to a consideration of the kind of moral learning integral to transgressive elements of drama work, particularly evident in Macbeth. When a child or teacher is being hot-seated as Macbeth, the more skilful they are at countering the accusations, the more enjoyable will be the improvisation. As with games, it is the structural features of drama, its game-like quality rather than its content that we should attend to here. It is just one of the many occasions in the lessons when children are being asked to think quickly and with cunning in drama. Other examples include the attempt to persuade Lady Higg to give food to Tinker Jim; arguments for or against Jim's imprisonment in the magistrate's court; arguing with the Emperor and the refuse collector; the attempts to rescue the slave from the patroller; the plans children develop to liberate the sea children.

'Wit' and 'cunning' may not readily spring to mind as parts of a curriculum for social and moral education. Let us then consider them as virtues of character, distinct from 'slyness' and 'deviousness', the opposites of which are 'dullness' and 'naivety'. To have children improvise and enact stories where brutish authority is challenged, defeated or made to look ridiculous through the exercise of wit and cunning rather than through a similar use of brute force is, I would suggest, a better model for moral action than is presented in many of the action films children are likely to be watching outside school.

Planning points

- Always have a wide resource of games at your finger tips and be aware of their different focuses for social and moral development.
- Games can be a good way of introducing drama work to those classes who are unused to it.
- Children can often benefit from being given simple guidance as to what constitutes positive behaviour for particular activities.
- Whenever possible, present rules and guidelines as a challenge rather than as a restriction.
- Remember that wit and cunning can be virtues, in the right situation.

Dialogue, dilemmas and passionate reasoning

Reason and emotion

Classroom talk normally consists of teachers asking questions, to which they already know the answers, and children answering them. More open-ended discussion does exist, of course, particularly in activities such as circle time, and older children might occasionally engage in debates to discuss issues such as whether certain kinds of hunting should be banned or whether it is cruel to make animals perform in circuses.

In drama, classroom talk is structured differently. For one thing, its heirarchical nature can be changed. The teacher may no longer be the one asking the questions; she may be silent or on the hot seat and in the firing line herself. Dramatic contexts open up different opportunities for children to engage with different kinds of talk but dialogue in drama lessons is at its most potent when it provokes children into arguing or discussing both rationally *and* passionately, engaging their emotions *and* their reason at one and the same time.

Throughout this chapter I have made many references to the development of children's feelings as an intrinsic part of their moral education but we would be wrong to persist in thinking of emotion and reason as two separate entities, the one cool and dispassionate, the other raw, natural and free-flowing. Emotions do not just happen. Children *learn* to feel in certain ways, which means that their feelings are rooted in reason. Experiences can teach a child to be frightened of her teacher's temper, to love books, to respect or despise authority. If the propensity for emotions such as love and fear are innate to us as human beings the objects of these emotions, *what* I come to love and fear, are learned. It is therefore quite natural for us to reason with emotion, passion even, when we are faced by moral issues, as such issues are emotive by their very nature.

One of the best ways of helping children learn to reason morally is, therefore, to engage their emotions with the issue under question. At its best, **improvised dialogue** in drama can achieve this by engaging children's feelings in the form of a moral response to a character whose actions or situation encapsulates such an issue. This response might be positive, by arousing the children's concern for the individual, or negative, by arousing their mistrust or their indignation. In both cases, children are being encouraged to *care* for their fellow human beings, for the difficult situations they find themselves in and for the consequences of their actions, whether good or bad. With children in the primary years, this can be most readily managed by the use of teacher in role.

Examples

Tinker Jim, Lesson 2. Children are concerned for Tinker Jim and argue with Lady Higg as to why she should give him some food.

Tinker Jim, Lesson 2. Teacher in role as the vicar tries to persuade Lady Higg not to give Jim any food. His attitude provokes children into indignation and hence into arguing against him.

Sweet Clara, Lesson 2. The shock of the doctor's insistence that the slave will return to Home Plantation as he can't be paid arouses great moral indignation in the children in role as slaves.

The Sea Woman, Lesson 2. The King's adviser is evidently holding something back when he refuses to say exactly what will happen to the sea children when they are removed from the island. As a result, the children do not trust him when he says they will be quite unharmed and this helps mobilise them into a rejection of his values.

Dialogue that is **crafted** rather than improvised engages children differently and does so at the point of performance. Such dialogue does not need to be naturalistic and it is often simpler to use a convention that creates a dialogue simply by being structured around oppositions.

Examples

Sho, Lesson 1. The poem the children help create and then perform emphasises the contrast between the angry and restless demons and the peaceful, constructive strength of Sho.

The Sea Woman, Lesson 1. The soundscape gives expression to an internal dialogue going on in the fisherman's head. Here the emotion evoked is one of pity and depends on the quality of performance.

Macbeth, Lesson 2. The conscience alley articulates Macbeth's internal dialogue before the murder of Duncan. Here the desired effect is a tingle of fear to evoke the horror of the act he is contemplating.

Dialogue as action

Good dramatic dialogue, whether improvised or scripted, is not the same as a conversation. It does not wander off at tangents but is structured around clear tensions and operates as action, inasmuch as it serves to clarify how characters see themselves and their particular situations and how they should act within them. This is important as it indicates that the moral stake of a dialogue in drama does not lie primarily in any decision that is made at the end of it but in the airing of the issues under discussion. It also matches the tensions produced by the most acute moral dilemmas that we face. These are not essentially about whether we should choose a 'good' over a 'bad' choice of action but about deciding which action to take when our sense of what is right pulls us in conflicting directions.

Examples
Sweet Clara, Lesson 2. The discussion with the doctor is ended with nothing resolved for the slaves. Any decision they now take will be significant but the point of the dialogue has been to *engage* the children in a moral discussion, not for them to win or lose it.
The Sea Woman, Lesson 3. When the King's adviser asks the children what he is to say to the King, the story is effectively over. The discussion will not shape what is to happen next but is itself an articulation of the island children's moral superiority over the figures of authority.

Different points of view

In a drama, we will often encourage different values and opinions to be expressed and often join in ourselves as teacher in role. It may well be that, as with the vicar in *Tinker Jim* or with the doctor in *Sweet Clara*, we are guiding the children into a moral response contrary to that we are expressing in the fiction. On the other hand, we may be trying to heighten children's sensitivities to the moral values, perceptions or struggles of those in different circumstances from themselves. This is often the overall aim of many drama lessons. Although schools will want their children to have a set of clear moral values, they will also want them to develop the imaginative capacity to understand that theirs is not the only perspective that matters. As primary teachers, we will want to discourage narrow-minded or bigoted attitudes that even young children can bring into the classroom with them.

It need not always be through dialogue, through talk, that we encourage what we might call a 'disposition of mindfulness' in children, a critical and sensitive awareness of other people's stances and of the environment around them. Such awareness in a drama lesson might best be achieved through the sequence of activities, so that one piece of action is followed by another that casts a different light or offers a different perspective on the issue. And this kind of awareness is as essential to children's development in literacy as it is to their developing moral understanding.

> *Example*
> In *The Sea Woman, Lesson 1*, after spending a number of activities exploring the injustice of the Sea Woman's situation, the children create an image that suddenly arouses pity for the fisherman. There is no question of the children feeling less sympathy for the Sea Woman but they are challenged to see her oppressor, too, as human and his actions as understandable if not excusable.

Planning points

- **Teacher in role** can be a most effective strategy for prompting children into active, improvised moral discussion.
- Strategies such as **conscience alley** can help you construct a symbolic dialogue with the class, to capture the different moral perspectives or possibilities for action at a particular moment in a story.
- There is no need for discussions over intractable moral dilemmas to reach closure; they are often best concluded on a note of indecision. Their aim is not to solve moral problems but to explore them.
- By sequencing activities to offer different perspectives on the same situation you can encourage children to be mindful of others and of the particular contexts within which they live.

Drama as a public and communal forum

The cultural and communal nature of moral values

It is often said that today we live in a climate of 'moral relativism'. As organised religion continues to decline and as our society becomes more pluralistic, more and more people choose for themselves the moral values by which they wish to live. In such a climate, it is argued, it becomes increasingly difficult for schools to teach moral values as there is no one, shared moral authority that schools can refer to.

Such a view may be widespread but it is flawed. At base, none of our moral values are the result of individual choice. They may be part of our individual identities but they are learned from and relate us to particular cultures, be they religious or secular, local or national. It is largely through stories that we learn these values, as the stories different cultures tell themselves about themselves tend to confirm a particular set of values and beliefs. Christianity has its own set of stories, as does Hinduism; as do varying national and local communities, and political and ethnic groups. Whatever our cultural and social roots – and they will be several – the values of these groups locate us within particular communities.

Schools are, first and foremost, communities and, as such, they embody a nexus of social and moral values. These values may be clear or ill-defined, coherent or contradictory; either way they will certainly be learned by the children who attend the school. It stands to reason, therefore, that a school must strive to be clear and coherent about the social and moral values it wishes to promote within its own environment. These can readily be described in terms that people from different cultural backgrounds can subscribe to. For example, if no one takes responsibility for their actions or shows respect for others in a school community then it cannot perform its educational functions. Such values are fundamental to its coherence. All schools will encourage the virtues of courage, honesty, duty, friendliness and loyalty and will reject the bully and the thief. Where individuals may differ is in how they recognise or define these qualities in particular circumstances or on the weight they place on particular values in relation to others. A young Hindu girl, for example, may have a different perspective on what filial duty means than the son of liberal white parents who sits next to her in class. Although a school will teach how the school expects such qualities to be practised within its own environment, it will also use stories to illustrate how they might look in different environments. Drama can help children investigate and scrutinise moral values in action; understand the effects that particular actions can have; and recognise that, although they will not always see things the same as others, they can still negotiate agreed ways forward.

Examples
The Frog Prince. Is the princess selfish? How does her selfishness affect others? In what ways do the children recognise selfishness?
Tinker Jim. Children are asked to reflect upon the drama regularly. What do we like and dislike about Lady Higg? Why? What do we think of Jim's stealing? These lead children to consider qualities of character they admire or dislike and to consider what they would see as justice in the case of Jim's punishment.
Sho Lesson 3. The children are asked to explain clearly to the refuse collector why he is wrong to do what he does.
Sweet Clara. Agreed rules are tested and the qualities of group loyalty are explored.
Macbeth. Macbeth's moral decline is regularly tracked, discussed and physically represented with reference to the virtues and vices his actions display.

Social roles and the virtues

As social beings, each of us is called upon to fulfil different roles. I am a son, a brother, a parent, a husband, a teacher and a friend and hopefully I try to be 'good' in all these roles. But the qualities that define this goodness may well differ from one role to the next; the qualities of a good teacher, for example, differ in many key ways from those of a good parent. Furthermore, a friend is expected to demonstrate a virtue such as loyalty in different ways and in different contexts than, say, a parent. This approach to understanding moral action in terms of *social ethics* immediately makes it something visible and open to discussion, despite its complexity. It is particularly relevant to drama's potential to introduce children to the domain of public morality, to ethical action in the world of work, of politics, of social life in general.

Children readily appreciate that certain ethical actions pertain to particular social roles; for example, they can readily talk about how a good student or a good teacher should behave. Most will also agree that a good doctor should put the care of his or her patients first, a good soldier should display bravery and loyalty, a good vicar should be charitable, a good parent should look after his or her children, a good ruler should be fair and just. It is this implicit understanding that enables children when working in drama to quickly tune into what they feel to be the rights and wrongs of a particular character's actions as they are displayed in particular contexts and circumstances.

Examples
Tinker Jim, Lesson 1. A child in role as Jim has the opportunity to tell the vicar in no uncertain terms *how* he should show charity to those in need.
Sweet Clara, Lesson 2. It is the fact that the teacher is in role as a *doctor* that does much to generate the heat in the dialogue, as most children do not expect doctors to put money before a patient's overall well-being.
Sho, Lesson 3. The children accept the Emperor's rule as he is evidently using his power for the benefit of his subjects and their environment.
Macbeth, Lesson 1. Children make still images to display all of Macbeth's virtuous qualities as described by Duncan.

Drama and the public sphere

The public forum for investigating and scrutinising social and moral values that drama can create is reflected in social life by such public spaces as churches, parliament and law courts. For children, the school is such a public space, particularly in its more formal aspects such as assemblies. These spaces are all, in their fashion, theatres, where the values that bind communities and societies together are displayed, scrutinised, discussed and debated. The formal nature of such public spaces can be mirrored in drama to create similarly formal spaces where social and moral values can be aired in a controlled manner. With older children, a tension that is both moral and dramatic can be motivated by the *disruption* of the protocol that normally governs agreed behaviour in these spaces. In engaging children in the airing of values in a public, dramatic forum, we are encouraging them to find a voice, to comment on, articulate or even challenge shared moral values, preparing them potentially to find such a voice in the public sphere of the world outside school. In this way, drama can contribute to the creation of active citizens ready to participate in a pluralistic, democratic society.

Examples
The Frog Prince, Lesson 3. The princess is on her throne and the children must try to use appropriate language when persuading her that her attitude to the frog prince is ungenerous.
Tinker Jim, Lesson 3. Using the formal setting of a magistrate's court, children discuss the nature of Jim's crime and debate the form of justice he deserves.
Sho, Lesson 3. When the children return to confront the refuse collector they are carrying with them a formal symbol of the Emperor's authority in the form of his scroll of law.
The Sea Woman, Lessons 2 and 3. The King's adviser always addresses the children in the formal space of the island school. In the final activity, children are encouraged to disrupt the protocol by challenging the King's moral authority.
Macbeth, Lesson 3. Children construct short scenes depicting the appearance of Banquo's ghost, highlighting how Macbeth's private sense of guilt disrupts the public space of formal kingly ritual.

Planning points

● Provide time and space for children to discuss the moral qualities they have demonstrated or witnessed in a drama, encouraging them to articulate how these qualities could be recognised in action.
● You can help children articulate ethical understandings by encouraging them to consider how the social role of a character relates to the actions they perform.
● Adopting the formal structures of public, social spaces such as courtrooms can provide children with opportunities to explore moral issues and, at the same time, educate them for future citizenship by introducing them to the conventions of language and social behaviour they call for.

Chapter 3
A whole-school framework

The argument of this book has not been that literacy and moral education are always best 'done' through drama, or that drama must of necessity directly support each of these curriculum areas. Obviously a drama methodology is not best suited to the teaching of, for example, the skills of reading and writing or to the teaching of moral codes. But where the teaching of drama *can* connect with and support the teaching of literacy and moral education, it is important for the school to document where and how for all three areas of the curriculum. The resulting whole-school framework will then help chart progression and continuity and assist with assessment.

A framework for literacy

For teachers in England these considerations are perhaps least problematic within the area of literacy. The National Literacy Strategy specifies what areas of literacy teachers ought to be covering with particular year groups. Every school will have its own system of monitoring and assessing the teaching of the literacy strategy and I am certainly not about to propose an alternative here. For the purposes of this book, however, three things are important:

● that teachers know where and how drama fits into the literacy strategy;
● that they know how it can support other English work;
● that the NLS targets met and/or supported by particular drama-centred projects are clearly signalled and assessed.

The National Drama Association have produced a very useful summary of the objectives of the NLS that directly relate to drama and this is included below as Figure 3.1. These include many of the objectives that relate to work with stories as well as those that relate directly to scriptwriting and plays. Although I have chosen to leave script work largely aside in this book, the lesson plans included show how a number of additional literacy objectives can be related to drama work. When planning your own drama projects, you may well begin with the list proposed in Figure 3.1 (pages 112–17) and then proceed to look for further, relevant objectives within those prescribed for the term's work.

References to drama in the National Literacy Strategy

Reception

Reception Year

Range
Fiction and Poetry: traditional, nursery and modern rhymes, chants, action verses, poetry and stories.

Text Level Work: Fiction and Poetry
7. to use knowledge of familiar texts to re-enact or retell to others, recounting the main points in correct sequence;
10. to reread and recite stories and rhymes with predictable and repeated patterns and experiment with similar rhyming patterns;

Writing
Composition
12. through guided and independent writing
● to experiment with writing in a variety of play, exploratory and role-play situations;
15. to use writing to communicate in a variety of ways, incorporating it into play and everyday classroom life, e.g. recounting their own experiences, lists, signs, directions, menus, labels, greeting cards, letters;

YEAR 1

Year 1 Term 1

Range
Fiction and Poetry: stories with familiar settings, stories and rhymes with predictable and repetitive patterns.

Non-fiction: signs, labels, captions, lists, instructions.

Test Level Work
Reading comprehension
6. to recite stories and rhymes with predictable and repeating patterns, extemporising on patterns orally by substituting words and phrases, extending patterns, inventing patterns and playing with rhyme;
7. re-enact stories in a variety of ways, e.g. through role-play, using dolls or puppets;

Non-fiction
Writing composition
16. to write and draw simple instructions and labels for everyday classroom use, e.g. in role-play area, for equipment;

Year 1 Term 2

Range
Fiction and Poetry: traditional stories and rhymes; fairy stories; stories and poems with familiar, predictable and patterned language from a range of cultures, including playground chants, action verses and rhymes; plays.

Text Level Work
Fiction and Poetry
Reading comprehension
8. to identify and discover characters, e.g. behaviour, appearance, qualities; to speculate about how they might behave; to discuss how they are described in the text; and to compare characters from different stories or plays;
9. to become aware of character and dialogue, e.g. by role-playing parts when reading aloud stories or plays with others;
11. to learn and recite simple poems and rhymes, with actions, and to re-read them from the text;

Year 1 Term 3

Range
Fiction and Poetry: Stories about fantasy worlds, poems with patterned and predictable structures; a variety of poems on similar themes.

Text Level Work
Fiction and Poetry
Reading comprehension
6. to prepare and retell stories orally, identifying and using some of the more formal features of story language;
11. to collect class and individual favourite poems for class anthologies, participate in reading aloud;

YEAR 2

Year 2 Term 1

Range
Fiction and Poetry: stories and a variety of poems with familiar settings.

Text Level Work
Fiction and Poetry
Reading comprehension
7. to learn, re-read and recite favourite poems;

Year 2 Term 2

Text Level Work
Fiction and Poetry
Reading comprehension
7. to prepare and retell stories individually and through role-play in groups, using dialogue and narrative from text;
8. to read own poems aloud;
9. to identify and discuss patterns of rhythm, rhyme and other features of sound in different poems;
10. to comment on and recognise when the reading aloud of a poem makes sense and is effective.

Year 2 Term 3

Range
Fiction and Poetry: texts with language play, e.g. riddles, tongue-twisters, humorous verse and stories.

Text Level Work
Fiction and Poetry
Reading comprehension
6. to read, respond imaginatively, recommend and collect examples of humorous stories, extracts, poems;

YEAR 3

Year 3 Term 1

Range
Fiction and poetry: plays.
Text Level Work
Fiction and Poetry
Reading comprehension
4. to read; prepare and present playscripts;
5. to recognise the key differences between prose and playscript, e.g. by looking at dialogue, stage directions, lay-out of text in prose and playscripts;

Writing composition
14. write simple playscripts based on own reading and oral work;

Year 3 Term 2

Range
Fiction and Poetry: oral and performance poetry from different cultures.

Text Level Work
Fiction and Poetry
Reading comprehension
4. to choose and prepare poems for performance, identifying appropriate expression, tone, volume and use of voices and other sounds;
5. rehearse and improve performance, taking note of punctuation and meaning;

Writing composition
11. to write new or extended verses for performance based on models of 'performance' and oral poetry read, e.g. rhythms, repetition;

Year 3 Term 3

Range
Fiction and Poetry: poetry that plays with language.

Text Level Work
Fiction and Poetry
Reading comprehension
7. to select, prepare and recite by heart poetry that plays with language or entertains, to recognise rhyme, alliteration and other patterns of sound that create effects;

Writing composition strategies
15. to write poetry that uses sound to create effects, e.g. onomatopoeia, alliteration, distinctive rhythms;

YEAR 4

Year 4 Term 1

Range
Fiction and Poetry: playscripts.
Text Level Work
Fiction and Poetry
Reading comprehension
5. to prepare, read and perform playscripts, compare organisation of scripts with stories – how are settings indicated, story lines made clear;

6. to chart the build-up of a play scene, e.g. how scenes start, how dialogue is expressed, and how scenes are concluded;

Writing composition
13. to write playscripts, e.g. using known stories as basis;

Year 4 Term 2

Range
Fiction and Poetry: (sci-fi, fantasy adventures).
Text Level Work
Fiction and Poetry
Reading comprehension
7. to identify different patterns of rhyme and verse in poetry, e.g. choruses, rhyming couplets, alternate line rhymes and to read these aloud effectively;

Year 4 Term 3

Range
Non-fiction
(i) Persuasive writing: adverts, circulars, flyers; (ii) discussion texts: debates, editorials; (iii) information books linked to other curricular areas.
Many of the areas included in this term's range of text level work for reading and writing can be delivered/enhanced through drama, especially with regards to the non-fiction elements.

YEAR 5

Year 5 Term 1

Range
Fiction and Poetry: play scripts.
Text Level Work
Fiction and Poetry
Reading comprehension
5. to understand dramatic conventions including:
● the conventions of scripting (e.g. stage directions, asides);
● how character can be communicated in words and gesture;
● how tension can be built up through pace, silences and delivery;

Writing composition
18. write own playscript, applying conventions learned from reading, include production notes;

19. to annotate a section of playscript as a preparation for performance, taking into account pace, movement, gesture and delivery of lines and the needs of the audience;
20. to evaluate the script and the performance for their dramatic interest and impact;

Year 5 Term 2

Range
Fiction and Poetry: longer classic poetry, including narrative poetry.
Text Level Work
Fiction and Poetry
Reading comprehension
5. to perform poems in a variety of ways;

Year 5 Term 3

Range
Fiction and Poetry: choral and performance poetry.
Text Level Work
Fiction and Poetry
Reading comprehension
4. to read rehearse and modify performance of poetry;

Writing composition
11. to use performance poems as models to write and to produce poetry in polished forms through revising, redrafting and presentation;

YEAR 6

Year 6 Term 1

Range
Fiction and Poetry: classic fiction, poetry and drama by long-established authors including, where appropriate, study of a Shakespeare play; adaptations of classics on film/TV.
Text Level Work
Fiction and Poetry
Reading comprehension
1. to complete and evaluate a novel or play in print and the film/TV version;

Writing composition
9. to prepare a short section of story as a script, e.g. using stage directions, location/setting;

Figure 3.1 Objectives that relate to drama adapted from the National Drama Association's publication *Reflections* published in Spring 1999

A framework for drama.

In *Beginning Drama 4–11*, Miles Tandy and I proposed a framework for primary drama based largely upon the DfE publication *Drama 5–16* but embracing the three categories of Making, Performing and Responding proposed by the Arts Council in *Drama in Schools*. We have since slightly modified this framework and I include it as Figure 3.2.

By the end of Year 2, children should be able to:
- play inventively and with concentration, both on their own and with others;
- understand and take pleasure in the difference between the conventions of dramatic play and the normal social conventions of the classroom;
- identify with characters and actions through role-playing, for instance in a dramatised story, and as spectators of a live performance;
- have the confidence and ability to put across a particular point of view;
- realise that the views of individuals do not always coincide;
- learn how to work together to solve human and practical problems;
- explore the difference between right and wrong in simple dilemmas posed through drama;
- make use of some simple performance conventions, e.g. mime; movement; stillness;
- actively take part in short, whole-class performance projects.

By the end of Year 6, children should be able to:
Making
- invent and develop new roles in specific situations;
- help create classroom dramas that explore particular issues with a practical, social or moral dimension;
- shape dramatic space and position bodies and objects meaningfully within it;
- sequence material for dramatic purposes, such as, for example, the clear presentation of a narrative;
- make symbolic use of objects, materials, light and sound;
- script simple dramatic scenes.

Performing
- use movement, voice and gesture in a controlled manner in order to convey meaning;
- sustain, in role or in performance, an intended atmosphere (such as humour) or an intended emotion (such as fear or anger).

Responding
- discuss drama and performance from a range of sources and cultures, including classroom drama, live performance (including Theatre in Education programmes), TV and film drama;
- recognise good work in drama through a critical observation of the characters created, the issues involved, the processes employed and the skills demonstrated.

Figure 3.2 Framework for primary drama

The end of Key Stage statements presented here are not in themselves learning objectives but they provide an achievable framework to which you can relate your own specific learning objectives in particular drama lessons. For example, the objectives for the Year 2 lessons around *Tinker Jim* relate to the statements for the end of Key Stage 1 as shown in Figure 3.3.

Statements for end of KS1	Learning objectives in 'Tinker Jim'
• identify with characters and actions through role-playing, for instance in a dramatised story, and as spectators of a live performance;	• to consider how costume and objects suggest character; • to participate in role and to engage in sustained role play; • to identify in role with the characters and actions of Tinker Jim, the vicar and Lady Higg;
• have the confidence and ability to put across a particular point of view; • realise that the views of individuals do not always coincide;	• to improvise dramatic play where different views are expressed, consistent with the characters in the the story;
• make use of some simple performance conventions e,.g. mime; movement; stillness.	• to develop and demonstrate some simple mime skills.

Figure 3.3 Statements for the end of Key Stage 1 linked to specific learning objectives

By recording and monitoring the spread of these objectives over particular drama projects, it is easier to plan for the breadth of drama experience to which children should be entitled.

A framework for moral education

This area is perhaps the most problematic of the three. At the time of writing, it is under review in England. National guidance is expected on personal, social and health education and you may wish to review the themes specified in these dramas in the light of this guidance when it is published. However, the 1991 publication by the Citizenship Foundation entitled *You, Me, Us! Social and Moral Responsibility for Primary Schools* did provide a very useful and well thought through pack, full of practical ideas and a variety of lesson plans. Considering this the most straightforward and accessible national guidance to date, I have used the framework it provides within the planning documentation in Chapter 1. In brief, they divide the social and moral curriculum into five areas to cover the themes of *Friendship; Rules; Property and Power; Respecting Differences; Community and Environment.* Within these particular themes, certain key moral ideas are clearly signalled as being conceptually at the heart of the work. It is these that I have adopted, with some slight adaptation, to provide the framework illustrated in Figure 3.4. The columns on the right of the Figure indicate that they are stated as learning objectives within the lessons provided in this book.

Social and moral themes Key ideas	Y1	Y2	Y3	Y4	Y5	Y6
Friendship						
Choosing friends	X					X
Qualities we admire						X
Loneliness, being without friends	X			X		
Peer pressure						
Trust and loyalty				X	X	X
Bullying					X	
Rules						
Laws and rules			X	X		X
Law breaking and wrongdoing		X	X			X
Blame, guilt and feeling sorry					X	X
Intention and responsibility					X	X
Rights and responsibilities			X	X		
Justice and fairness		X		X		
Motives for behaviour	X	X	X	X	X	X
Property and Power						
Equality and inequality		X		X	X	
The value of property	X			X		
Ownership of property					X	
Sharing and not sharing		X	X			
The difference between power and authority					X	X
The difference between revenge and justice						X
Stealing		X				
Punishment		X	X			X
The consequences of crime		X	X			X
Victims of crime						X
The qualities of leadership			X		X	X

Respecting Differences							
Respect for self							
Similarities and differences between people						X	
Respecting racial and cultural differences					X	X	
Respect and concern for others	X	X	X		X	X	
Empathy for those in different circumstances	X	X			X	X	
Gender roles					X	X	
Discrimination and prejudice		X			X	X	
Community and Environment							
Working together				X	X		
Responsibility for the environment				X			
Belonging and not belonging						X	
Group responsibilities				X	X		
Individual responsibilities				X			X

Figure 3.4 Framework for social and moral curriculum (adapted from Citizenship Foundation's publication *You, Me, Us!*)

If you cast a critical eye over this list, you will doubtless notice that its underlying philosophical thrust is not entirely congruent with my own, as expounded in Chapter 2. In particular, it concentrates on social themes much more than it does on the language of the virtues. However, it is well beyond the scope of this book to propose a fully developed and coherent social and moral curriculum. My intention has been to show how drama can work alongside broadly consensual aims that will characterise such a curriculum. The 'fit' between the drama lessons and the framework of *You, Me, Us!* is not a perfect one; but, for the most part, as Figure 3.4 shows, it is close enough. And, although some of the ideas are not covered within the dramas, it is clear that most are.

Of course, some schools will already have very well-developed frameworks with additional priorities to those specified here. If a school is affiliated to a particular religious denomination for example, the moral precepts of this faith will be integral to what the school sees as children's moral development. Furthermore, in the event of further guidance from the government, the likelihood is that this framework will have to be altered. It is presented, therefore, not as a blueprint but as an illustration of how it can be relatively simple to document drama's contribution to a specified curriculum for social and moral education.

In addition to these specific themes and ideas there are, of course, skills and attitudes that drama can help develop over the long term, as explored in the last chapter. These are integral to the demands of participating in dramatic activity and deal with children's capacity for negotiation and compromise for example, and their ability to work within shared rules of behaviour. Rather than being restated as general objectives for specific drama projects or lessons, these are best included in an overall rationale for drama's contribution to the social and moral development of children. Such a rationale, no longer than a page of A4 at the most, could be presented as a series of bullet points under the heading: *How drama contributes to the social and moral education of the children in this school.* It could then be attached to the school's policy statements for drama and for social and moral education so that school governors and parents, as well as teachers, can understand the principles that underlie social and moral education through drama.

Documenting objectives and assessment criteria

Assessment criteria for drama and social and moral education are possible, though they will be different in form from those subject areas where learning can largely be measured by whether children get things correct or not. Here you will need to make informed judgements based upon careful observations of what the children do or say. It will of course be impossible to evaluate every child in every lesson but, by focusing on different children each lesson, you will be able to note achievement over a period of time. Written and visual work (including video and photographs) can also be used for assessment purposes.

It is important to be specific about what your objectives for the project are and how you are going to judge children's learning against them. These can then be documented on a sheet of A4, as in Figure 3.5. Of course, you may, as the project progresses, judge some of these objectives to be more significant than others with different classes of children. But the documentation remains an open account of those areas that will be touched upon. In this way, you can not only monitor and plan for learning in all year groups, but you can share and make public your aims for drama education and clearly demonstrate its additional value for children within the areas of literacy and social and moral learning. This is, I would argue, important not only in terms of accountability but in order to gain the trust, understanding and support of parents and governors.

Title of unit: *THE SEA WOMAN* Taught in: Year 5, Term 2	
NLS targets T1; T2; T3; T5; T8;T11; T13; T14	
We are also expecting the children:	The children will show what they have learnt/ are learning:
In drama • to use still image work to convey a specific, emotional charge; • to use materials to create symbolic meaning; • to create a simple, whole-class performance using sound and movement; • to sustain a role and contribute to the maintenance of dramatic tension in whole class and group work; • to speculate and contribute to the development of plot; • to use language to persuade; • to devise and present a piece of drama with the emphasis on gesture and mime	• through showing the worst moment in the story for the Sea Woman • through creating a series of moving images in groups using netting material; • through participating in the performance; • through their contributions in the scenes with the King's adviser and in small group role play; • through their responses to the question 'What should happen next?'; • when evaluating if and how the children manage to convince the fisherman of the danger to his children; • through their participation in a short play showing how the sea children manage to escape.
In social and moral education • to develop their powers of empathy; • to explore ideas of belonging and not belonging; • to consider the relationship between intention and responsibility; • to examine symbolically issues of racial and cultural difference, prejudice and discrimination; • to show concern for others; • to develop an understanding of how power can be abused; • to consider issues of friendship, loyalty and human rights.	• through creating still images and performance work that demonstrate an understanding of the Sea Woman's sufferings; • through discussing and presenting images of the Sea Woman's entrapment; through sharing personal stories; • through image work exploring the fisherman's responsibilities for the events of the story; • through their comments in and out of role when discussing the demands of the King to remove the sea children; through their story writing; • through their actions and comments in role when attempting to save the sea children; • through their work in role with the King's adviser; through their comments out of role; through their story writing. • by evaluating why, as children of the island, they helped the sea children.

Figure 3.5 Documenting objectives

Appendix 1
Games used in the lesson plans

Assassin

This is a great favourite with upper primary children but it requires a strong element of self-control and agreed safety procedures. It is very good for exploring tension and fear. The children spread out in the hall space and close their eyes. You silently touch one child on the shoulder. They are now the 'assassin'. On the word from you, children begin to walk slowly through the space, keeping their eyes closed all the time. The aim is to meet as many people as possible, hopefully avoiding the assassin. To meet someone you reach out and take them by the arm and ask the question 'Assassin?' to which you will receive the reply 'Assassin!' At this you move on and try to meet someone else. Meanwhile, the assassin, too, is moving through the space with their eyes closed and meeting people but saying nothing throughout the game. So, if on asking the question 'Assassin?' you hear no reply, then you ask it again 'Assassin?' just to make sure. If you still hear no reply then you must die very loudly before retiring to one side of the hall. The game concludes when the assassin has murdered everyone in the class!

Farmer and the Fox

The children stand in a circle. One of them is chosen to be the Fox and stands apart from the circle, facing away from it. A child is then chosen to be the Farmer and the Fox's prey (a cuddly toy, for example) is placed in the centre of the circle. The Fox must now enter through a gap in the circle, not knowing which child is the Farmer. As soon as the Fox touches the prey the Farmer can begin to give chase. If the Farmer touches the Fox, he immediately becomes the Fox himself and the chase continues. Whoever manages to make it back through the gap in the circle to the Fox's den wins the game.

Grandmother's footsteps

Children stand at one end of the hall while the teacher or a child stands at the other, facing the wall. The children move as silently as possible towards the wall opposite but at any moment the teacher or child will suddenly turn around and look. If they see any child move, that child must go back to the wall and start again.

I went to the market

The children sit in a circle. The game begins by one child saying 'I went to the market and I bought some eggs' (or fish, or potatoes, etc.). The child next to them must repeat the sentence but say that they bought something different. It is completed when every child has had a turn.

Keeper of the Keys

The children sit in a circle and a volunteer sits blindfolded on a chair in the centre with a rolled up piece of sugar paper in their hand. A large key or other object (such as a book of spells) is placed under the chair. A child in the circle volunteers to attempt to retrieve the object. If the keeper in the centre manages to hit the child with the paper, they must return to the circle and another child can have a try. Silence provides the tension for this very popular game.

Knights, Dogs and Trees

Select a child to face the wall and be caller. The rest of the class now runs round the space until the call 'Freeze!' At this point the children must freeze in the shape of a knight, a dog or a tree. Now ask the caller to choose and call out one of these shapes. Should they call out 'Knights', the knights remain frozen while the rest of the class resume running through the space. At the next call of 'Freeze!' the knights may remain frozen as knights or may choose to change their shape. As soon as all the children are once more frozen into their chosen shape, the caller calls out again and the game continues.

What do we like about X?

Children sit in a circle. A child ('X') volunteers to leave the room and the teacher asks the class to help them make a list of the things that we like about X. We can limit this to the five best things about X. When the child comes back into the room they can try to guess who said what about them or simply bask in the praise!

Appendix 2
Drama conventions referred to in this book

Acting out. This is when children improvise around a situation, often in small groups. The intention is not necessarily for them to show their work at the end. If you do want this to be a prelude to some small performance, then see the section on **performance** and **short play** below.

Collective role. The role of a character is played by more than one child simultaneously. Each child might express a different aspect of the child's personality.

Conscience alley. The class is formed into two lines between which a character can walk. As she walks down the 'alley' her thoughts are spoken by the rest of the class. She may be on her way to some event in the drama or she may be faced with a difficult decision.

Forum theatre. Individual members of the class are chosen to enact a particular scene. The rest of the class observe but both actors and observers can stop the action at any point to ask for or give guidance as to how the scene might be developed.

Hot seating. Someone (either teacher or child) assumes a role and is questioned by the rest of the group. The role may be signalled by sitting in a particular seat (the 'hot seat') or perhaps by wearing an item of costume or holding a particular artefact.

Line of allegiance. At some point in a drama the teacher asks children to form a line according to their opinion or feelings about a particular character or event. 'If you feel a lot of sympathy for X at this point, stand at this side of the room; if you feel no sympathy at all, stand at the opposite side. If your feelings are not that extreme, place yourself in between at an appropriate place in the line.'

Mapping the story. The idea here is not to make a map as such but to draw one large, collective picture that illustrates the setting, characters and events of the story in the way the children see fit.

Meeting in role. The whole class is in role as a group that needs to meet to hear news, report on progress or make decisions. The teacher may or may not be in role with the class depending on whether she needs to influence the direction the meeting takes.

Mime. This can range from simple, improvised movement, as in Year 1, Lesson 1, or more carefully crafted uses of movement and gesture as in Year 5, Lesson 3. It may be accompanied and supported by teacher narration.

Narration. The teacher may use narration to introduce, link or conclude action. It might be used to slow and intensify action, such as when the children make their way to the fisherman's cottage in Year 5, Lesson 2. It may mark the passage of time, as in Year 4, Lesson 2, or introduce the next stage of a drama.

Outside eye. This is useful for older children when they are devising short pieces for performance. The 'outside eye' is a child who watches the action in order to comment on it as an outsider. They can make suggestions and offer advice when the group cannot reach agreement or decide what will work best. The important principle is, however, that they do not speak unless asked to. The outside eye can be a member of the group who is temporarily outside the action; or a member from another group whose work the teacher has deemed to be satisfactorily finished, as suggested in Year 6, Lesson 3.

Parallel scenes/images. Two or more scenes that would in reality happen in different places and perhaps at different times are played next to each other. The action in one can be 'frozen' and the other brought alive to explore the connections and tensions between them.

Performance. There will be times in drama lessons when you judge it desirable for children to work in groups and craft their ideas into a **short play**. With primary aged children, this is best kept very short and they will benefit from very clear structures and points of focus. It is often a good idea for groups to perform in sequence with no talking or moving other than from the performers themselves until all groups have finished. This introduction of performance discipline helps children respect their own and one another's work.

Preview. Just as previews of films arouse our curiosity and interest without giving too much away, a teacher might choose, before beginning a drama, to present an image from the forthcoming story and ask children to speculate upon its meaning.

Sculpt/model. A child volunteers to be the clay while another child sculpts or models the clay into their idea of how a particular character might appear at a certain moment in the drama. It is often a good idea to encourage a number of different interpretations.

Snapshot. Like a short play only shorter! Groups rehearse and perform a brief and focused piece of action. The context, characters, setting etc. must already be very clear from previous work.

Snippets of action. After acting out their ideas, rather than asking the children to craft them into a short play, the teacher can ask groups to choose what they consider to be the three most significant moments of action. They can then rehearse and perform these three snippets of action – three or four seconds each – using words and movement. The other groups can then piece together what has happened, speculate on why those particular moments were chosen and/or comment on how the ideas were presented.

Sound collage. Sounds are made, often by the whole class using voice, body and/or instruments, either to accompany actions or to create atmosphere.

Still image/tableau. Groups work to create an image of a moment in time using their own bodies. Often it will represent people 'frozen' in the middle of some action but it may represent a more abstract idea, such as the virtues of Macbeth as described by the king in Year 6, Lesson 1.

Story wand. The story wand – often a walking stick – is a device to get children to spontaneously act out a story as you narrate it. They sit in a circle and volunteer to take on the role of characters as you introduce them and to do the actions and say the words suggested by the storyteller. As you wave the wand across the space the characters disappear back into the circle and, as you resume the story, different children can volunteer to take their turn.

Storytelling. Exactly what it says! You can use your storytelling skills to interest children in stories that you want them to work on, as in Year 1 and Year 5 in this book. You can also use them to move the plot along at points within a drama, perhaps in role, as with Year 6, Lesson 3.

Teacher in role. The teacher takes a full part in the drama, often using her role to manage the drama from within the action. Teacher roles can have a variety of statuses, offering different power relationships within the group. A simple item of costume or a prop can help younger children understand when you are in or out of role.

Thought tracking. The private thoughts or reactions of a character are spoken publicly, either by the character herself or by other participants in the drama. It might be used when the action is frozen or used in conjunction with still images.

A short bibliography

Some more story books for exploring moral issues and doing drama

Years 1 and 2
Catkin by Antonia Barber and P. J. Lynch (1994), London, Walker Books.
Charlie's House by Reviva Schermbrucker and Niki Daly (1989), Cape Town, David
    Philip Publishers.
Giant by Juliet and Charles Snape (1989), London, Walker Books.
Jack and the Beanstalk by John Howe (1989), London, Little Brown and Co.
Red Riding Hood by Christopher Coady (1991), London, ABC Publications.
Two Can Toucan by David McKee (1986), London, Beaver Books.
Where the Wild Things Are by Maurice Sendak (1975), London, Bodley Head.
Witch, Witch, come to my Party by Arden Druce (1998), Swindon, Child's Play.

Years 3 and 4
Clever Polly and the Stupid Wolf by Catherine Storr (1995), London, Young Puffin.
Higglety Pigglety Pop! by Maurice Sendak (1991), London, Bodley Head.
Lon Po Po by Ed Young (1989), New York, Putnam and Grosset.
Outside, Over There by Maurice Sendak (1993), London, Harper Collins.
Seasons of Splendour by Madhur Jaffrey (1992), London, Puffin.
Snow White by Josephine Poole and Angela Barrett (1993), London, Red Fox.
Storm Boy by Paul Owen Lewis (1995), Hillsborough, Oregon, Beyond Words
    Publishing.
The Little Match Girl by Hans Christian Anderson (n.d.), Leicester, Galley Press.

Years 5 and 6
Clockwork by Philip Pullman (1997), London, Corgi Yearling.
The Hob Stories by William Mayne (1991), London, Walker Books.
I am the Mummy Heb Nefert by Eve Bunting (1997), Ontario, Tundra Books.
The Enchanter's Daughter by Antonia Barber (1987), London, Jonathan Cape.
The Sweetest Fig by Chris Van Allsburg (1993), London, Andersen Press.
How to Live Forever by Colin Thompson (1995), New York, Alfred A. Knopf.
The Bone Keeper by Megan McDonald and G. Brian Karas (1999), New York, DK
    Publishing Inc.
Maudie and the Green Children by Adrian Mitchell (1996), Surrey, Trade Wind Books.

Books on primary drama teaching

Bolton, G. (1992) *New Perspectives on Classroom Drama.* Hemel Hempstead: Simon and Schuster.

Kitson, N. and Spiby, I. (1997) *Drama 7–11.* London: Routledge.

Morgan, N. and Saxton J. (1987) *Teaching Drama.* London: Hutchinson.

Neelands, J. (1991) *Learning Through Imagined Experience.* London: Hodder and Stoughton.

Readman, G. and Lamont, G. (1994) *Drama – A Handbook for Primary Teachers.* London: BBC Educational.

Tarlington, C. and Verriour, P. (1991) *Role Drama.* Ontario Canada: Pembroke.

Winston, J. and Tandy, M. (1998) *Beginning Drama: 4–11.* London: David Fulton Publishers.

Woolland, B. (1993) *The Teaching of Drama in the Primary School.* London: Longman.